GETTING IT ISSUED

SECOND EDITION

BY HANK GEORGE & JOHN J. KRINIK

The
NATIONAL
UNDERWRITER
Company

The National Underwriter Co. • PO Box14367 • Cincinnati, OH 45250-0367

ISBN: 0-87218-262-2

Second Edition

Printed in U.S.A.

Dedication

This book is joyously dedicated to two great genres of insurance professionals: those who sell our products (producers), and those who make them salable (underwriters).

Table of Contents

CHAPTER 1

The Mutuality of Our Endeavors

The first edition of *Getting It Issued* began with this anecodotal reminiscence:

Some years ago, at a local underwriters' club dinner meeting in the Midwest, a tall, fair-haired actuary, trying to share his vision of our industry's future with a hundred well-fed, only slightly drowsy home office underwriters, made a statement something like this:

> **"Effective interaction between producers and home office underwriters is the key to the success of our life insurance distribution system."**

That was then. Today that actuary would probably say:

> **"Effective interaction between *applicants, producers and home office underwriters* is the key to the success of our life insurance distribution system."**

There you have it. The key change in the way insurance is being sold and purchased is the more active involvement of the applicant. New distribution systems, with or without agent intervention, are the future of the insurance business. Banks are contracting with agencies to provide insurance sales and service to depositors. Agency and insurer web sites are now a key part of insurance marketing strategies in the 21st century. Today's prospect thinks he has more control over his buying decision – and he does!

The reasons this book was written and the reasons you bought it were to:

- **acquire knowledge to more effectively prepare clients for underwriting;**

- **embrace more effective strategies; and**

- **"Live long *and prosper!*" (Thank you, Spock.)**

Why is the home office underwriter important to the applicant and producer? Because the underwriter is positioned at the critical juncture of new business income and profitability, matching the risk to the premium charged. There are three sources of profitability for a life insurer:

1. **investment yields;**

2. **expense savings; and**

3. **mortality gains.**

Companies look to mortality and morbidity gains – in other words, to the results of careful underwriting – as a major contributor to profits. No profits = no company = no producers.

Our life insurance system is anchored by the concept of risk classification and, thus, by the carrying out of the risk selection process which we call "underwriting." To make life insurance affordable and attractive to clients, life expectancy must be in line with the mortality assumptions used to set premiums. Stop underwriting and this would change abruptly. Life insurance would need to be repriced in order to avoid insolvency as persons "incentivized" by illness purchased insurance. The new, higher prices (required to pay claims of the worsening "at risk" population) would drive away healthy buyers. Life insurance would become unsalable.

Home office underwriting makes insurance affordable for most buyers. Producers, therefore, not only need underwriters but they have a vested interest in contributing to the efficiency of the underwriting process. This book will show you how to accomplish that goal.

Why is the producer important to the home office underwriter? First and foremost, the producer generates insurance company income. If there is no income, how is the underwriter's salary paid?

At the beginning of the last decade, reengineering was a major preoccupation of the industry. With the rethinking and the reorganizing came the recognition that the producer was the home office underwriter's *client* just as the insurance buyer was the producer's *client*. This had profound implications on how the underwriter's performance was evaluated. Both philosophically and practically in day-to-day activities, the career-conscious, upward bound, home office underwriter would promote the interests of his client.

As the 21st century dawns, the insurance industry is preoccupied with mergers, acquisitions, consolidation and market shrinkage. The home office underwriter now recognizes the ultimate truth: the insurance buyer is *everyone's client*. It is the job of the underwriter and producer, working together, to serve the needs of the client in a responsive manner. If you fail the client, he now has other choices that didn't exist as recently as the middle of the last decade.

What is the best thing an underwriter can get in terms of recognition for a job well done? Positive feedback, to his boss's boss, from a leading producer. It could be a letter to the senior vice president of operations proclaiming that the underwriter saved a case or snatched a sale from the jaws of a competitor through prompt action, innovative intervention or diligent facilitation.

Producers and underwriters serve *clients* together. This is a partnership that will continue to be of profound importance to the success of the life insurance business in the 21st century.

How Underwriting Performance Is Evaluated

Service and Speed

You know better than anyone in the insurance business how important it is to receive prompt application approval and policy delivery. Each day that goes by after the client has completed the application gives the client an opportunity to reconsider his buying decision. Even if you took a prepayment, a lengthy delay in delivering the policy can create enough doubt in the client's mind to provoke him to refuse the policy and ask for a refund. When faced with competition from another agent, being second to deliver a policy is often a guarantee you will lose the sale.

Underwriters are acutely aware of the urgency to get policies approved and issued. After all, underwriting departments constantly receive inquiries from agents about pending applications. At many companies, electronic tracking systems are used to provide you with up-to-the-minute status of your applications. Today's management systems provide reports about overall time service patterns to company executives so when serious delays seem to occur, corrective action can be taken immediately. In days past, something as simple as a special colored envelop for new business applications might have been the solution for reducing file setup delays. Today, a sophisticated computer program might need to be tweaked.

Some of the common, new business service measurements are:

- **days from application date to date received in the home office;**

- **days from receipt in the home office to the first review by an underwriter;**

- **days from the first review to ordering of the initial requirement(s);**

- **days from the ordering of requirements to their receipt in the home office;**

- **days from receipt of the last requirement to final action (approve or decline);**

- **days from underwriter approval to policy mailing.**

From company to company, the choice of what service times are acceptable may vary greatly. Those decisions can be affected by the:

- **type of product;**

- **average face amount of the application;**

- **type of agency system (branch management, career agency, personal producing general agency, brokerage);**

- **geographic market;**

- **level of technology employed between field, home office and service vendors for submission and processing of applications and requirements.**

When performance evaluations for underwriters are done, chronic service delays may have an adverse impact on that employee's rating. To the extent that underwriters have a natural motivation to act promptly on your submitted business, personal inattention to pending applications is the exception, not the rule. However, underwriters must balance the demand for prompt turnaround time with the appropriate analysis of risk information. For that reason, many companies that have not begun using automated and/or expert technology have "jet issue" units for screening uncomplicated applications. Their experienced underwriters only review files with complex risk factors and/or assorted requirements for which detailed analysis is necessary.

Nevertheless, most time service delays caused by "snail mail" (post office) have been eliminated through the use of electronic transmission of both applications and vendor requirements. Many vendors have established web sites at which requirements can be ordered. You may use a laptop and modem to transmit applications to the company(ies) you represent. Most service vendors (laboratories, paramedical services and inspection companies) use electronic transmission of completed blood and urine results, examinations and inspection reports. For example, pen-based technology allows handwritten responses to examinations and electronic signatures to be transmitted instantaneously to underwriting departments. Laboratories provide overnight express service for blood and urine samples to be sent from the paramedical examiner to the laboratory. You and the client benefit from the use of overnight express and electronic transmission of such requirements.

As more health care providers computerize their patients' medical records, attending physician statements will be transmitted electronically to insurers. Of course, proper authorization forms and signatures are still necessary but, in many jurisdictions, electronic transmission of these may become accepted, too. Some service vendors provide Attending Physician Statements (APS) services whereby they either photocopy or electronically scan patient records at the office of the health care provider. Then the copies are sent either by overnight express mail or electronically imaged by modem to the insurer.

Many insurers have begun making widespread use of personal history telephone interviews (PHI) with the client by utilizing either vendor or home office employees. The detailed and well-designed questions used for PHIs often permit decisions to be made without ordering APSs.

Profitability

You and your clients benefit from three primary responsibilities of insurance company management:

1. **wise investments;**
2. **prudent underwriting; and**
3. **sound expense control.**

Underwriting quality and profitability are measured differently for the same reasons that were enumerated in the previous discussion that outlined a company's choice of acceptable service times. Additional factors include;

- **age and economic demographics of the market;**

- **stock versus mutual organization;**

- **corporate strategies related to aggressive versus conservative pricing of impaired risks;**

- **company size and surplus position;**

- **reinsurance arrangements – automatic/facultative thresholds and cost of reinsurance;**

- **past, present and future dividend philosophies;**

- **expense control strategies and cost/benefit analyses of underwriting requirements;**

- **technology capabilities; and**

- **regulatory compliance.**

The mortality tables in use today affect the pricing of life insurance products with dramatically low mortality ratios and very narrow mortality margins. Increasing life expectancies drive insurers to find innovative ways to lower premiums and reduce expenses. Insurers are aggressively raising the thresholds at which they obtain many underwriting requirements – inspections, exams, electrocardiograms (EKGs) and APSs.

The protective value of biochemical tests so outweighs the costs that most insurers raise their limits for other requirements in order to justify the continued use of those tests, especially in the preferred pricing environments. In many companies, at ages under 65 and at amounts for millions of dollars of life insurance, biochemical profiles and nonmedical applications are so reliable they are the primary means to achieving underwriting profitability.

However, in the older age markets, and for very large amount applications (defined differently by various insurers), APSs, examinations and inspections still offer substantial protective value. PHIs might permit limited ordering of APSs, but detailed medical histories on applicants over age 65 still allow the most accurate risk assessment and favorable underwriting possible. For large amount applications, the direct interview inspection report still affords a means to minimize adverse selection, especially through the verification and corroboration of information provided by the applicants during the application process.

How Risk-based Pricing Allows Widespread Availability and Affordability of Insurance

Did you ever think that underwriting makes insurance more difficult to sell and buy? If so, you are not alone. Any agent who has had to deliver a rated policy or explain a declination knows the frustration inherent in these situations. Yet, some historical perspective is helpful to your own understanding and will also help you articulate to clients how risk-based insurance pricing actually helps them.

Several hundred years ago, trade and professional guilds that provided a death benefit to their members would deny coverage to those in obviously bad health. At the death of a member, they often collected a levy from surviving members to assure payment of the full death benefit promised to the widow. Early insurance companies in the 17th and 18th centuries that insured applicants without underwriting soon discovered, through their excessive claims, that not everyone who applied could be insured. Since most insurers were local companies, they began to require that applicants appear in person before the board of directors, which usually included one physician. Applicants also had to sign statements such as: "I am not given to drink or other intemperance...I am not subject to any disorder which might tend to the shortening of my days..."

At the beginning of this century, most insurers still evaluated life insurance applications on an accept or decline basis. Sixteen substandard risk classifications, let alone today's preferred pricing, did not exist. Impaired risk underwriting was still a novel concept in the late 19th century and most insurers simply did not feel they had adequate mortality statistics to experiment with pricing beyond the standard class. However, the old Equitable issued policies rated 11 percent over standard for gout or hernia as early as 1762. Over a century later, in 1892, medical directors and actuaries combined efforts to build mortality tables for common risk factors of the day – being overweight, high blood pressure, gout, etc. By 1913, the first Medico-Actuarial Mortality Investigation was completed and companies began to formulate ratings for the most common substandard conditions.

From these beginnings, and after hundreds of years of experience, insurers today can accept over 90 percent of all applicants at standard rates. Substandard premium coverage is offered to about 7 percent of all applicants, thereby leaving uninsurable only 2 percent to 3 percent of all who apply. In fact, with the experimental impaired risk underwriting programs operating today at many insurance companies, some of those "uninsurables" succeed in obtaining affordable coverage. Risk-based insurance pricing and the practice of risk classification allows each member of the insured lives pool to contribute a premium reasonably commensurate with their mortality risk. Not only is that the most equitable manner on which to base insurance premiums, but it also allows the greatest number of applicants to have access to affordable life insurance.

The Life Underwriter as a Professional

"Personally, I think underwriters are the most important people in the life insurance organization."

–William W. Fenniman, CLU, ChFC
Branch Manager, ManuLife
Boston, Massachusetts
Proceedings of the 49th Annual Meeting
Institute of Home Office Underwriters

In a typical life insurance company, three professions have a direct impact on the risk selection process:

1. the actuary;
2. the medical director; and
3. the (lay) underwriter.

Actuaries set the premium structure and substandard rating classes. They may also be involved in mortality studies, cost-effectiveness assessments of underwriting requirements, etc.

Historically, medical directors had a much broader role than they typically have today. Where it was once the rule rather than the exception for the outcome of a large or complicated case to be decided by a medical director, much of the accountability for decision-making on difficult cases now vests entirely with the underwriter. The medical director is primarily a consultant, sought out for medical expertise. In addition, medical directors interpret chest x-rays and electrocardiograms, contribute to the setting of medical underwriting standards and practices and assist in establishing medical underwriting requirements. In most North American life companies, however, the medical director does not have final accountability for the underwriting decision on any individual case. That accountability rests solely with the life underwriter.

The Underwriter Has the Final Say on the Case

The foregoing discussion of the role of the medical director in a contemporary life insurance company has, in my view, two important implications for producers.

1. You need to deal *directly with the underwriter* on the case at hand. The underwriter has the final authority. Even though, in your experience, some cases may have been arbitrated by the medical director or the underwriting department head, the fact remains that the underwriter makes the final decision and, 99+ percent of the time, that decision stands.

2. As a financial services professional, you have pride in your work and confidence in your abilities. You would take it poorly if a client went to your general agent for a second opinion about your advice (or worse, to try to get a better deal). The underwriter is also a professional. Producers who work *through the underwriter* build a relationship of respect and mutual trust.

Deal Directly With the Underwriter

Life insurance underwriting is a unique profession. There is no institution of higher learning in the world where one may matriculate with a major in underwriting. Nonetheless, the successful underwriter will have extensive knowledge in a variety of fields of studies, including medicine, law, accounting, business analysis, statistics and so on.

Indeed, the uniqueness of the underwriting profession is inherent in what the underwriter must know. He must know more about the heart than anyone *except* physicians and cardiac intensive care nurses; more about certain aspects of contract law than anyone *except* lawyers. Someone once described life underwriting as the "Renaissance occupation." That's a good analogy.

Since one cannot major in underwriting, life underwriters typically come from a wide-range of backgrounds. One expects to see a disproportionate number of underwriters with B.B.A. degrees or B.S. degrees with a pre-med focus. In fact, in a large underwriting department, the opposite is apt to be true. Liberal arts degrees abound. Three of this author's closest friends – all underwriting department heads in large companies – have undergraduate degrees in French, English Literature and Nursing, respectively.

It has been said that life underwriting is both an art and a science. The ability to pull together a broad range of medical, financial, occupational and avocational information and make a decision that will withstand scrutiny and challenge from many quarters is one that cannot be conferred solely by formal education or on-the-job training. It requires what one might call a "sixth sense." An underwriter friend from Winnipeg maintains it is *prima facie* evidence that underwriters are "right brain" people.

Perhaps this explains why some of the most talented underwriters in North America do not have university degrees or formal letters after their names. In some cases, they started their careers as clerks or even messengers, ultimately becoming underwriting professionals. They have those endowments that, simply stated, make them great underwriters.

Guiding Principles for the Underwriter

It is the responsibility of each underwriter to:

- **Act promptly, while exercising sound, objective and consistent judgment, in making underwriting decisions.**

- **Follow established risk classification principles that differentiate fairly on the basis of sound actuarial principles and/or reasonably anticipated mortality or morbidity experience.**

- **Treat all underwriting information with the utmost confidentiality and use it only for the express purpose of evaluating and classifying the risk.**

- **Comply with the letter and spirit of all insurance legislation and regulations, particularly as they apply to risk classification, privacy and disclosure.**

- **Avoid any underwriting action that is in conflict with the obligation to act independently and without bias.**

- **Act responsibly as an employee with scrupulous attention to the mutual trust required in an employer-employee relationship.**

- **Provide information and support to sales personnel in order to help them fulfill their field underwriting responsibilities in selecting risks and submitting underwriting information.**

- **Strive to attain Fellowship in the Academy of Life Underwriting, maintain a high level of professional competency through continued education and help promote the further education of all underwriters.**

- **Maintain the dignity and sound reputation of the underwriting profession.**

- **Increase the public's understanding of underwriting by providing information about risk classification.**

The Life Underwriting Profession

Like their professional peers – the actuaries and medical directors – life underwriters also have professional associations. In the United States, two underwriter organizations are national in scope and membership:

1. **The Home Office Life Underwriters Association (HOLUA); and**

2. **The Institute of Home Office Underwriters (IHOU).**

In Canada, the national association is known as:

- **The Canadian Institute of Underwriters (CIU).**

Each of these groups has an annual conference of two (CIU) or three (HOLUA, IHOU) days' duration, typically convened in late spring (HOLUA) or autumn (CIU, IHOU).

There is also an extensive network of regional, state/provincial and local underwriters clubs in North America. In the United States, four regional meetings are held annually, designated as the New England Home Office Underwriters Association (HOUA), the Southeastern HOUA, the Midwestern HOUA and the Western HOUA. In Quebec, the Association Quebecoise Des Tarificateurs-Vie (AQTV) convenes an annual French language conference.

At last count there were 33 state and local life underwriters clubs in North America. Some of the largest, located in major insurance centers such as Toronto,

Hartford/Springfield, MA and Minneapolis/St. Paul, routinely attract several hundred attendees at a midweek dinner meeting.

The underwriting profession has made tremendous strides in the last two decades in the development of components essential to any profession; distinct credentials specific to life underwriting, continuing education opportunities and a professional journal.

In the mid-1970s, the HOLUA and the IHOU formed a joint undertaking known as the Life Underwriting Educational Committee which directs the activities of the Academy of Life Underwriting (ALU). The Academy, in turn, is made up of three components:

1. **a professional education program leading to the Fellow of the Academy of Life Underwriting (FALU) designation;**

2. **a seminar program; and**

3. **the journal of the Academy entitled *ON THE RISK*.**

To earn the coveted FALU designation, an underwriter must pass two extensive examinations and then either write a research paper or, in lieu of the paper, sit for a third comprehensive examination. In addition to those requirements, the underwriter must also pass a number of exams from both the Life Office Management Association (LOMA) and the Chartered Life Underwriter (CLU) programs. There is an intermediate designation, the Associate of the Academy of Life Underwriting (AALU), awarded to those who complete all of the program's components except the research paper or third examination. As of 1999, over *600* underwriters had attained the FALU designation.

The Academy's seminar program offers underwriters an opportunity for continuing education. In a typical year, the Academy will sponsor three seminars in North America. Each seminar consists of two days of, primarily, lectures by medical directors, underwriters and others, on medical, lay and financial underwriting topics. In addition, specialty seminars have been offered on financial underwriting, disability income and underwriting management. The registration fees are set much lower than comparable seminars marketed to the industry, thus assuring that ALU seminars are, invariably, full houses. Brokers and underwriters from brokerage firms have attended ALU seminars over the years. Details of upcoming ALU seminars can be found in each issue of *ON THE RISK*.

When the first issue of the quarterly underwriting professional journal *ON THE RISK* was mailed to members of the HOLUA and the IHOU in 1984, the journal consisted of eight pages of articles. Fifteen years later, the average issue is nearly 100 pages with a variety of papers and articles on topics of interest to life, health and disability underwriters, medical directors, actuaries, claims managers, marketing executives, brokers and other industry professionals. Subsidized by an extensive advertising program, *ON THE RISK* is affordably priced and claims 4,000 subscribers with a pass-along readership estimated in excess of 10,000 persons in fifty countries on six continents.

In 1997 in Mexico City, and in 1999 in London, the International Underwriting Congress was convened for underwriters from around the globe. This Congress is held every 30 months in a great international city.

Speaking about the international dimensions of the life underwriting profession, it should be noted that there are no fewer than three major underwriters clubs in England, another in Scotland and, at last count, similar organizations in Mexico, the Caribbean region, South Africa, the Philippines, Hong Kong and Malaysia. In Australia, the Australian Life Underwriting and Claims Association (ALUCA) convenes a biennial three day meeting. Life underwriting is, in every way, an international profession.

Sources of Information About Underwriting

The producer's first choice as a source of underwriting information should always be the "field underwriting guide," or on-line equivalent, distributed by his insurer. This guide (assuming it exists; if it does not, someone should build it!) is unique among reference sources because it focuses on the perspective of that insurer. A generic definition of what constitutes a "key person" or an acceptable blood profile is, obviously, less relevant to the producer than how *his company* defines those terms.

Rule # I: Know Your Own "Field Underwriting Guide"

Unfortunately, the readings for producer-focused education programs, such as CLU, ChFC (Chartered Financial Consultant) and LUTC (Life Underwriter Training Council) contain little information in any detail about underwriting. The Life Office Management Association (LOMA) in Atlanta has a textbook for new underwriters entitled, *Underwriting Life and Health Insurance*. It is a handy, one volume reference for producers, officers, managers, etc. For more information call LOMA at (770) 951-1770.

ON THE RISK journal, mentioned previously, is the premier source of contemporary information about life and disability underwriting. Each issue contains a wide-range of papers and articles on medical, lay and financial underwriting topics. These are written by veteran underwriters, medical directors and actuaries, including *ON THE RISK*'s team of contributing editors. *ON THE RISK* is very affordable which might explain why its roster of producer subscribers has grown steadily in recent years. Producers working in the older age market, with larger amounts and substandard risks (especially in brokerage), will find the modest outlay for *ON THE RISK* is a wise investment. For more information about subscribing to *ON THE RISK*, please visit www.ontherisk.org or contact:

Dennis Fagan, FALU
Circulation Manager
P.O. Box 267
Claymont, DE 19703-0267
e-mail address: ontherisk@aol.com
Phone: (302) 421-8956
Fax: (302) 421-8964

Underwriter ALERT and *Hank's JournalScan* are bimonthly newsletters devoted to hot topics of interest to underwriters. Whereas *ON THE RISK* is formatted as a professional journal with many lengthy articles, *Underwriter ALERT* and *Hank's JournalScan* consist of short, to-the-point reporting. For more information about subscribing to *Underwriter ALERT* and *Hank's JournalScan*, please contact:

John Krinik
Publisher
Underwriter ALERT / Hank's JournalScan
P.O. Box 2990
Binghamton, NY 13902-2990
e-mail: ualert@ProNetisp.net
Phone: (607) 724-3992
Fax: (607) 724-0041

The premier medical underwriting textbook is *Medical Selection of Life Risks* authored by two renowned medical directors: R.D.C. Brackenridge of Mercantile and General Reinsurance (London) and John Elder of Transamerica Life (Kansas City). Within the 900+ pages of this tome, every significant aspect of insurance medicine is dissected and discussed. Although written for medical directors and senior underwriters, this book is remarkably understandable. The book is published by Stockton Press, 257 Park Avenue South, New York, NY 10010.

There are many medical reference books published for physicians and nurses. Most are far too detailed and technically written to be effectively used by producers. Probably the best of the lot is *The Merck Manual of Diagnosis and Therapy* published by Merck & Co., Inc., of Rahway, New Jersey. Producers working in the substandard market, who must frequently meet the challenge of delivering rated policies, might wish to examine this book as a possible adjuvant reference course. It can be viewed at many larger book stores and in all book outlets at medical schools. It is inexpensive ($30 per copy) and easy to use.

BROKER WORLD magazine is another source of underwriting information, especially for producers writing impaired risk business. Each issue contains several articles related to underwriting and the November 1999 issue focused on risk appraisal topics. Just that issue alone would have been worth the annual subscription price. *BROKER WORLD* is published monthly. For more information about subscribing to *BROKER WORLD*, please phone: (800) 762-3387.

In recent years, the Home Office Life Underwriters Association has been reaching out to agents, general agents and brokers as potential members. Affiliate membership status, available to nonunderwriters, is surprisingly inexpensive and offers five payoffs worth considering:

1. **A bound copy of the annual PROCEEDINGS of the HOLUA conference that is loaded with the text lectures, panels and workshops about underwriting.**

2. **All members receive ON THE RISK journal.**

3. **Discounted registration fees for the annual conference, which invariably counts a cohort of producers among its attendees.**

4. **The intangible, but not at all insignificant, benefit of showing your interest in and support for the underwriting profession.**

5. **The membership directory that lists over 1,000 members with titles, addresses and telephone numbers.**

For more information about HOLUA membership, visit www.ontherisk.org/
holua/ or contact:

The Home Office Life Underwriters Association
Phone: (770) 984-3715

The Joint Risk Classification Committee (JRCC) of HOLUA and IHOU was
formed in 1987 to help promote greater public understanding of how and why
insurers use risk factors as the basis for insurance premiums. To achieve that
goal, the JRCC has published a four-color brochure, "Risk Selection: The Fair
Approach," that makes a convenient and informative handout for clients. Also
available is a short video originally produced by the American Council of Life
Insurance (ACLI) that illustrates how risk affects premiums. For more
information visit www.ontherisk.org/jrcc/.

Selection and Antiselection

The earliest underwriters during the 17th and 18th centuries were also the
sales agents. That is, they signed their personal acceptance of the risk on the
contract. They evaluated the risk in keeping with their own mortality
assumptions for the premiums collected and their own sales objectives for their
companies. In essence, these "field underwriters" selected the risks their company
desired to insure. Risk selection performed by insurers today has the same
objectives:

- **to insure lives that will produce the mortality objectives set
  by the company when they established their premiums; and**

- **to satisfy the sales goals set by the company in order to
  assure the financial strength needed for future claims and
  benefit payments.**

Unlike those early practitioners, today's underwriter rarely, if ever, sees a
client. Applications and assorted other documents form a picture of the client
in the mind's eye of the underwriter. Still you, as an insurance agent, always
have the best opportunity to evaluate your clients as they sit across from you,
answering questions and discussing their needs.

In the mid-90s, the Houston Association of Life Underwriters published a
booklet entitled *Are You in Compliance?* These professional life insurance agents
decided they were the best qualified insurance professionals to address the
industry problems that fall under the heading of "market conduct." In the section

devoted to "Underwriting," these words of wisdom appear: "An agent who compromises part of the underwriting process with false or misleading information, as it pertains to the prospective insured, is creating potential wealth for litigating attorneys."

Antiselection is not just some esoteric underwriting jargon; it describes the essence of insurance. That is, insurance is designed for those risks that are unforeseen and unanticipated, such as premature death. When an applicant anticipates premature death because of specific knowledge known only to him and not the insurer, the insurer is being selected against. The playing field is no longer level and the insurer is being "gamed."

For most underwriters, any discovery of lack of candor by the client in response to the application creates an aura of suspicion. Unfortunately, if the information was so obvious that the agent could not possibly have mistaken it, his reputation will suffer. Two examples: many underwriters have encountered applicants who actually weighed 300 or more pounds, but the recorded weight on the nonmedical questionnaire was less than 200 pounds. Or the client who had a severe, crippling disorder, but who had all the medical questions answered as if he was in perfect health.

An agent's reputation is very difficult to repair after an obvious lack of candor involving agent complicity. Application fraud, which implies intent to deceive the insurer, can result in rescission of a policy and might create a liability problem for the agent. Some insurers may consider contract termination. Individual circumstances and the agent's track record will dictate whether severe penalties are appropriate. After all, what if an innocent beneficiary is deprived of life insurance proceeds after an insured's death because of material misrepresentation on the application? What if the agent participated in the deception? Litigation against the agent may be inevitable. This scenario is becoming more common with smoker misrepresentation.

Certainly, you do not need that kind of trouble. Your job is difficult enough without risking your relationship with the insurers you represent. The underwriters' trust and confidence in your professionalism takes time to earn. Rather than trying to "sneak one past" the underwriters, it is always better to work with them and develop all the details necessary to give them the most accurate picture possible of the risk. Your client's forthright disclosure of all medical or nonmedical details will put the underwriter at ease and create a climate of trust. In those ambiguous situations where a clear-cut decision is not obvious, you will probably be rewarded with the benefit of the doubt and a placeable offer.

"Does It Make Sense?"

In 1970, the late Charles A. Will, Vice President, Cologne Life Reinsurance Company, wrote a textbook for underwriters entitled *Does It Make Sense?* (The National Underwriter Company, Cincinnati, Ohio). Although no longer in print, the title is part of the jargon of underwriters everywhere. This question is worth asking yourself before you submit any application to the underwriters. If you were sitting at the underwriter's desk and received those documents, would it all make sense? Having never met, seen or spoken with this client, would you have an accurate and clear picture of the person, the policy and the risk? If, after answering those questions, the application does make sense, then send it to the underwriter.

SMART...VERY SMART
by John J. Krinik

(Reprinted with permission from *PROBE*, February 24, 1992, PROBE, Inc., Route 1, Box 88a, Nanjemoy, Md. 20662.)

A recent issue of an insurer's monthly marketing publication demonstrated one marketing officer's savvy human relations skill. In his column, he described how the company is known for its quality products and competitive premiums. But the executive said he often hears complaints about the company's underwriting..."too tough and takes too long." Agents sometimes tell him that fear of losing certain cases prompts them to send apps elsewhere.

Instead of launching into a contrite explanation of the company's underwriting policy, this marketing executive simply published two letters from agents. Those letters praised the superior efforts of three home office underwriters of separate applications to quickly process, helpfully explain, and ultimately issue placeable offers. The underwriters, whose names were published, couldn't help but be proud that their work on behalf of these agents had been publicly recognized. You can bet that they won't soon forget who wrote those letters.

Most underwriters languish in professional anonymity until something goes wrong. Then there's an angry phone call or vitriolic letter or appeal to senior management... sometimes all three. Letters of praise are as rare as snowflakes in August. But, as every agent and marketer knows, praise is a powerful motivator.

It's the home office underwriter's lot in life to deal with adversity. Adversity skills that help underwriters to explain why the requirement can't be waived or why the rating can't be reduced aren't part of most underwriters training. Agents, on the other hand, are professionally trained to overcome objections. These differences in professional training can become acute in the presence of an intractable underwriting problem that pits a "salesperson" against a "technician."

Today's corporate emphasis on customer service, and insurers' late recognition of agents as customers, has helped to improve the climate for agent/underwriter relations. But the explosion in biochemical testing and the strain on profit margins creates tension and uncertainty in the sales environment. Insurer downsizing trends create tension and uncertainty in home offices. Human relations skills are necessary to maintaining smooth working relationships between agents and underwriters.

The marketing executive and the agents mentioned at the beginning of this article demonstrated such skills. The reward will be more placeable offers and mutual profitability for those agents and that insurer.

Smart...very smart.

Additional Reading

1. *Are You in Compliance?*, Houston Association of Life Underwriters, 1994.

2. Shepard, P. and Webster, A., *Selection of Risks*, Society of Actuaries, 1957.

CHAPTER 2

The Client Wants to Apply

Anticipation of Underwriting

Successful people usually have a highly developed sense of intuition. It is based upon an ability to embed their experiences into memory, combine them with learned knowledge and skills and readily apply them as current situations require. Hockey legend Wayne Gretzky, when asked how he got into position to score so many goals, replied, "I go to where the puck is going to be." And he knew where it was going to be two or three passes early.

After insurance agents have gained a few years experience, medical or nonmedical problems and their likely underwriting outcome should be anticipated. A final underwriting decision cannot be known to an agent because of the number of sources of information that are not seen by the agent: laboratory tests, inspection reports and personal history (telephone) interviews (PHIs), motor vehicle reports (MVRs), attending physicians' statements (APSs) and so on. Yet, the agent who has taken the time to ask the applicant details about his health, regardless of the need for an insurance exam, is in control of the application process.

Acceptability of Ratings, Riders or Modifications to Prospective Clients

Imagine that you see an advertisement for an item at a particular price and then drive to the store to buy it. How do you feel if the salesman says, "I'm sorry, we're out of that product, but let me show you this equally fine product," with the implication being that the substitute product is at a higher price? You probably have a low opinion of the store's operational management or feel hoodwinked. Intentional bait and switch tactics are not only unethical, they are probably illegal.

Think about that if your initial premium quote to an applicant is innocently lower than the final premium after underwriting. Clients are often suspicious about a rated policy. That reaction is especially likely if you were aware of an underwriting risk factor when you took the application but didn't discuss the possibility of an extra premium charge or modification with your client before leaving the sales interview.

Therefore, we believe that taking a nonmedical questionnaire, even though a paramedical or even a full MD exam will be performed later, is in your best interest. It assures that there will be no medical history surprises. It redflags problems which need special intervention, like a pre-application/submission telephone conversation with the Underwriting Department. It allows you to be in control and to influence the underwriting process in a positive manner.

When you anticipate an extra premium charge or other modification, you can discuss that possibility with your client. You can prepare him for a higher premium and, thus, evaluate his capacity for accepting a rated policy. If the sale was driven by a maximum premium outlay, you can evaluate the potential for a reduced benefit or for choosing a different product. Most importantly, you enhance your professional credibility with the client. Additionally, with market conduct issues impacting our industry of late, an *anticipatory* sales strategy could pay unexpected dividends!

Calling the Underwriter Before Submitting the Application

Although some companies still discourage direct producer calls to home office underwriters, most insurers prefer that their agencies call about significant medical and nonmedical risks when the producer suspects that high ratings or disapprovals might be in the picture. The same is true for unusual or complicated underwriting scenarios (the insured residing overseas is a good example). Large amounts of coverage might also warrant a call ahead, especially when applications are being submitted to multiple carriers at the same time. Some companies even welcome preliminary calls where "preferred" or "standard" is the only placeable premium, although medical or nonmedical factors pose a potential problem.

Before the call, you should develop as much detail as possible from the client (consistent with the recommendations elsewhere in this book for specific impairments, nonmedical or financial factors). Many companies would prefer to minimize the expense of attending physician statements on inquiries that are highly unlikely to result in a placeable offer. So a preliminary telephone call from a fully prepared producer may be welcomed. However, those insurers who encourage formal "trial" or preliminary applications instead of phone calls still need your diligent attention to obtain the details as completely as possible.

Never send a trial application with just a doctor's name and address and the name of the impairment. When you do you are actually sending this message to the underwriters: "I'm too busy to be bothered developing the details of this case. Order the APSs and figure it out yourself." If you do not care any more than that, why should the insurer?

Issuing and Explaining Receipts: Conditional and Temporary

You know how important it is to close the sale with a check from the applicant. It demonstrates your client's intention to fulfill the requirements and accept the policy. However, it is equally important that the terms of the receipt you give in return for the check are fully understood by the applicant.

The wording of conditional receipts varies from insurer to insurer, but typically the policy offered must be "approved as applied for" without additional ratings or modifications in order for the conditional coverage to be in effect. Also, the requirements must usually be completed for such coverage to be in effect, especially for any necessary examination. Finally, most conditional receipts have a time limitation after which the conditional coverage expires and the premiums are refunded, perhaps 60 or 90 days from the date of the receipt. There is usually an amount limitation, too, – $250,000 is common – regardless of the face amount applied for on the application. If you do not clarify such conditions with your applicant, you and your company are vulnerable to expensive and unfavorable litigation in the event of a claim denial for death or disability occurring prior to policy issue.

The "temporary" receipts being used by many insurers are an attempt to provide unconditional coverage during the short time period prior to policy approval. Typically, two or three questions relating to recent hospitalizations or a very serious medical history such as cancer, heart attack, AIDS and so on, must be answered in the negative to allow you to take the applicant's check and immediately put temporary coverage in force. There is usually a maximum death benefit, but it is often more than the maximums contained in the conditional receipts. Your failure to ask the questions, but still take the check, might result in a refund and delay while the company awaits the return of the original receipt. Worse, the client may change his mind about the insurance.

Informed Consent / Authorization Forms / Confidentiality

Unnecessary underwriting delays can be due to incomplete or unsigned authorization forms. Inspection problems can be due to a client's lack of prior knowledge about the investigation. You can avoid such delays if you take the time to review and explain informed consent and disclosure notices.

More importantly, though, confidentiality of personal information has become a critically important issue as genetic advances provoke discussion of the appropriate uses of genetic information by employers and insurers. Your sensitivity to the privacy concerns of your clients will be best illustrated by your patient explanations of the authorization form, the Medical Information Bureau (MIB) Pre-notice and Fair Credit Reporting Act (FCRA) disclosure forms.

After all, before you allow any invasive medical procedure to be performed on yourself, you are likely to want to know what the purpose is and why it is necessary. In fact, it is your legal right as a patient in most jurisdictions. That is the origin of the informed consent forms that your clients must read, understand and sign before any laboratory tests are performed. The examiner or technician is usually responsible for those forms.

Informed consent principles also apply to the authorization forms which give the applicant's permission to the insurer to contact medical and nonmedical sources for information about your client and to share that information with reinsurers. You are required to not only explain the authorization form, but also to explain and deliver MIB Pre-notices and FCRA disclosure forms to your client. If you were in your client's place, you would certainly want to be informed about the insurer's access to and use of your personal medical and nonmedical records, along with any investigation of you that is being conducted as a condition of your insurance purchase.

Contestability / Legal Compliance / Litigation

Your clients deserve to understand the contestability clause and its potential impact on their beneficiaries in the event that the insurer discovers during a claim investigation that there was material misrepresentation by the insured when applying for the policy. Some insurers have even begun putting warnings on their application forms about the loss of coverage that might result due to fraudulent answers to application questions. Moreover, as a result of recent state level insurance fraud legislation, insurers may be able to initiate legal action against applicants who have submitted applications found to contain overt misrepresentation, whether a policy was issued or not–whether a claim for benefits was made or not.

Legal compliance is not a new issue, but it has become a top agenda item for regulators and insurance company management in the aftermath of the market conduct crisis. Extremely severe penalties and multi-million dollar fines get the attention of boards of directors and senior executives of insurers. New business departments at the home offices are often expected to be the enforcement agents of your collection and proper completion of mandated disclosure forms.

Some laws are worded to prohibit you from taking an application or submitting an application without the presence of the pertinent forms. Only you can take steps to avoid the unnecessary delays occasioned by the return of application papers or suspension of application processing simply because legally required forms were either missing or improperly completed. Do not waste anyone's time, especially your own, appealing to an underwriter to waive a legally required form. Just get it right the first time.

Litigation enriches attorneys. It can also ruin insurance agents' careers and deplete policyholder surplus and stockholder earnings. There is no room in the insurance industry for inattention to the laws governing insurance transactions let alone for illegal activities. Fundamentally, your focus should always be on serving your clients with good faith and complete integrity. It is in your self-interest to act in their best interest.

The Cover Letter

"A good cover letter can make or break a case."

Victoria Van Dusen
Diversified Brokerage Services, Inc.

There are realities about the underwriting process that we never think about. An example is the fact that the insurance application gathers very little of the kind of detail that underwriters really need to make decisions on sensitive or complicated cases. Another is the fact that underwriters virtually never see (and rarely speak to) insurance applicants, instead relying entirely for their perspective on what is recorded on the application and in the personal history interview (PHI).

Remember, it is the underwriter's initial impression of the risk that sets the tone of the case and guides the underwriter in ordering elective requirements.

Since the application is a "bare bones" skeleton of the facts of the case and because initial impressions are crucial, most successful producers have acquired a constructive habit – the habit of writing cover letters.

A "cover letter" may assume many forms. In today's world of communication alternatives, it could, literally, be:

- **a formal, typed letter on your personal letterhead;**

- **an e-mail; or**

- **just a brief, handwritten note appended to the application!**

The key is that this thing we choose to call a "cover letter" be a meaningful, informative communication between the producer (who wrote the case) and the home office underwriter (who will assess its insurability).

The cover letter tells the underwriter what he needs to know to get his job done as quickly as possible, with as few requirements as possible. It amplifies what is said on the application papers. Quite literally, it tells (in the words of that famous Chicago radio journalist) "the rest of the story."

There are two species of cover letters. The first one contains productive information that helps the underwriter see the case in perspective, that guides him in his review of the risk. The other one is what we like to call "snake oil!" It is not really relevant to the issue(s) at hand, rather, it blows smoke, makes inflated statements and negatively polarizes the reader (or worse, arouses his suspicions!).

A story might help put the value of cover letters in perspective. Twenty years ago, as an Underwriting Consultant in the Large Risk Division of Northwestern Mutual Life, I [HG] saw an application for life insurance on the life of a fortysomething Boston lawyer. Because of his age and the amount of insurance for which he applied, both a resting electrocardiogram and a chest x-ray were required.

The electrocardiogram was not normal. The proposed insured had a resting heart rate of only 42 beats a minute. This is called sinus bradycardia (slow heart rate). The average, healthy adult has a resting heart rate in the 60s – twenty beats higher!

In addition to his slow heart rate, the ECG also revealed what is called a first degree heart block. In plain English: the electrical impulse which moves through the heart msucle, inducing it to contract and to pump blood, was, shall we say, *undermotivated.*

The barrister's insurability, already compromised by the ECG findings, was dealt an even greater blow when his chest x-ray showed mild heart enlargement. The risk was assessed as Table H (as in "Ha! Ha! Ha! You expect me to deliver this?").

About a week after the policy was mailed, I got a rather agitated telephone call from the producer. He was frustrated. I recall tucking the phone under my chin and, while continuing to work, yelling, "NO!!" from time to time through the receiver.

The producer would not hang up so I decided it was time to bring it to a close. "You have sixty seconds," I said, "to make your case!" His response unraveled the mystery. "I can't believe a man who finished the Boston marathon last year is a Table H!"

Neither can I.

This gentleman was a long distance runner, one of those people who runs forty miles a week…just for fun! The ECG and chest x-ray abnormalities, suggestive of cardiac illness in your garden variety "couch potato," represented what cardiologists call the "athletic heart syndrome." In other words, the harmless physiologic effects of intensive athletic conditioning and superb cardiorespiratory fitness!

Table H? Quite the contrary. "Standard" in 1975; probably "super-preferred" in many companies today!

What was the key to the case? It was the fact that this client was a highly conditioned athlete who ran marathons.

Think about it. Is there a "marathon running" question on *your* company's application? How is an underwriter supposed to distinguish a genuine athlete from someone whose idea of "exercise" is bench pressing quarter barrels of beer into his pickup truck to take to a tailgate parrty?

Can you see how a cover letter might have avoided the problem encountered on this case? If not, read this chapter again!

Some Cover Letter Topics

- **Any discussions you have with an underwriter *prior to submitting the case*; full details, as you understand them, of anything that is agreed to; requirements that are waived or modified, tentative appaisals of the risk, etc.**

- **Justification of the amount of insurance applied for (versus the insured's income), purpose of coverage (e.g., Key Person), etc.**

- **Explanation of the reason(s) underlying special ownership, beneficiary or payor requests.**

- **Census of related applications, especially if they are not submitted simultaneously.**

- **Amplification of sensitive medical histories, such as alcohol or drug abuse and psychiatric impairments.**

- **Criminal records, bankruptcies and related financial difficulties and adverse driving records.**

- **Further details on unusual or potentially ratable occupations or avocations.**

- **Full details of all medications taken by the client, *both* by prescription (which should already be recorded on the Part II) *and* over-the-counter. The latter may include an aspirin a day, herbs and other alternative medical remedies, performance-enhancing dietary supplements, oral** contraceptives, hormone replacement therapy, megadoses of antioxidants and so on.

- **Details of current or planned future foreign travel to areas of possible underwriting concern. Clients residing in foreign countries that presents requirement completion obstacles.**

- **Any other potential problem with completing the underwriting requirements including a *full explanation* of what problem(s) are anticipated.**

- **Details of any competitive situation. How can the underwriter help you win?**

- **A candid, up-front statement of the special importance of this case to you (e.g., qualifying for MDRT or a sales contest award). Is there a deadline? How can the underwriter help you?**

The cover letter is your personal communication with your underwriter. It can be as long as it needs to be, in whatever detail the situation mandates. Brevity is not always an asset in this regard.

In some cases, the information you provide in a cover letter may represent a statement from the proposed insured which, in turn, may need to be made part of the contract. In those cases, consider submitting the cover letter *over the insured's signature*, dated and witnessed by you with your signature. Follow any specific rules your company has for such situations. You will probably speed up approval of the case or might also avoid later delivery requirements.

Cover letters move business. Successful producers whose business seems to breeze through Underwriting are usually *chronic* cover letter writers. Frustrated producers, on the other hand, who like to blame Underwriting for everything from lost sales to global warming, typically never heard of 'em!

Reinsurance and How It Affects Underwriting

Most direct writing insurers have "treaties" with reinsurers for the purpose of limiting the amount of the risk they accept on an individual life. Smaller companies may retain less than $100,000 per life and reinsure policies that exceed that level. Medium-sized companies may retain amounts up to, or in the vicinity of, $1 million per life. The largest companies retain amounts approximating $20 million or more.

"Automatic" reinsurance limits are set at amounts mutually acceptable to the direct writer and the reinsurer. A smaller company might be able to underwrite applications on its own authority up to $500,000 even though it retains only $100,000 at its own risk. An application at that company for $750,000 would require "facultative" underwriting done by the reinsurer, meaning that they would need to see all the application papers and evidence of insurability before accepting their portion of the risk. This transaction is usually invisible to you and your client if the approval is prompt and the policy is issued.

Yet, when the reinsurer evaluates the risk differently than the direct insurer, several things can happen. Additional requirements may be requested to allow the reinsurer an opportunity to price the risk at the same rate as the direct insurer. Or the direct insurer may "shop" the file to other reinsurers with whom it has treaties in the hope of receiving a more favorable evaluation. Retention limits are usually approved by the board of directors and often filed with the state insurance departments. The direct insurer cannot exceed its retention on any single case in order to place the coverage at a lower rate.

Another use of reinsurance "shopping" occurs when the direct insurer cannot make an offer within its retention that you can place. In an attempt to help you deliver a placeable offer through your primary company, the underwriter will send copies of the underwriting evidence to his reinsurers. The reinsurer who delivers a placeable offer will probably reinsure the entire risk but, once again, it will be transparent to you and your client...unless new requirements are necessary.

Life reinsurers may be paid a premium by the direct insurer comparable to a one-year renewable term rate. For some products, the reinsurer will "co-insure" and receive a portion of each premium dollar the direct company collects. Among other factors, the overall reinsurance rates are negotiated based upon the amount and quality of business expected from the direct insurer. Even if you sell a very large premium whole life policy, the reinsurer may not share in the substantial cash flow unless it negotiated a generous coinsurance treaty. Reinsurers that receive the lowest possible premium the direct insurer could negotiate under the treaty may still assume the largest portion of the risk. This is important for you to understand because it affects the aggressiveness of the reinsurance underwriters. The direct insurer may find the potential premium as attractive as you do, but the reinsurer is, quite naturally, focused on the mortality risk.

How does this affect you? If you have not done a thorough job developing the evidence of insurability that the direct insurer needs, including all the relevant financial documentation appropriate to large amounts of coverage, then the reinsurer will be even less inclined to look favorably upon the risk. If the reinsurer requests additional evidence in an attempt to evaluate the risk more favorably, you and your client should cooperate fully.

Agents who split very large coverage amounts among several direct insurers can create reinsurance capacity and underwriting administration problems. The same proposed insured's application might be concurrently submitted to different direct insurers by one agent, inadvertently tying up capacity among the reinsurers who may have seen the same life from different sources. Of course, even reinsurers have retention limits and use other reinsurers as "retrocessionaires" (direct insurers "cede" coverage to reinsurers who, in turn, retrocede to other reinsurers). However, the number of available reinsurers is a fraction of the number of direct insurers. Consequently, it is not difficult to "lock up the reinsurance market" for a large enough case. To correct this problem, a preliminary call to your primary direct insurer to "reserve facilities" with the reinsurers and to act as the "lead" reinsurer is appropriate.

Sending your client's application to multiple brokerage agencies or insurers to "see if it sticks" anywhere is a surefire way to create reinsurance problems. Make sure that all insurers understand that you are "splitting" the case among specific companies rather than "shopping" the case. If either the direct insurers or reinsurers misunderstand your intentions, late explanations and assurances may fall on deaf ears. Be perfectly clear about your intentions on the first submission of the client's application papers.

Chapter Notes

1. "How to Write a Cover Letter," Victoria Van Dusen, *Broker World*, Vol. 19, No. 11, November, 1999, page 42.

CHAPTER 3

Completing The Application

Theory A versus Theory B

A 1994 Life Office Management Association (LOMA) survey asked insurers why applications for life insurance are not issued. This is what the survey respondents reported:

File closed for missing requirements	38%
Application withdrawn by client	26%
Declined by underwriter	26%
Postponed by underwriter	10%

Fact: most decisions by clients to discontinue underwriting ("application withdrawn by client") can be directly linked to frustration or impatience with underwriting delays and other problems in requirement acquisition. Therefore, two out of every three times that an application does not result in a deliverable policy, it is because of *problems with requirements*, not because the client is uninsurable!

These are *avoidable* problems. *They do not have to happen to you!* This whole book is about seeing to it that they don't.

Read on…

There are three possible solutions to the problem of the lost sales addressed by the LOMA survey. Which do you think will be the most effective?

1. **Send these findings, with an angry letter demanding immediate action, to the senior vice president of insurance operations (with a "courtesy" copy to the chief underwriter).**

2. **Build a shrine to the Goddess of Requirement Delays.** Insist that all associates leave offerings of food or, better, precious stones to appease this horrific deity.

3. **Examine your attitudes about underwriting.** Do you subscribe to Theory A or Theory B?

Theory A holds that the home office underwriter is an intractable nitpicker. It suggests that he pours over every word on the application and on each of the requirements looking for any flyspeck which he can blow out of proportion. The end result, of course, is either (best scenario) more requirements or (worst scenario) adverse action.

The producer must, therefore, take appropriate countermeasures: keep information on the application brief and vague; choose less inflammatory words like "cyst" or "fatigue" rather than requirement-provokers like "tumor" or "depression"; misspell key medical terms to further muddy the waters. Above all, *never*, ever amplify *any* medical or financial history until you are compelled to do so in the face of threatened file closure!

There are two kinds of underwriting requirements:

1. **age/amount; and**

2. **elective.**

Age/amount requirements, as the name implies, are based on the client's age and/or the amount of insurance for which he applied. The number of such requirements per case tends to increase both with the client's age and with the amount of coverage sought.

Age/amount requirement limits are carefully set to collect the minimum amount of essential information needed to underwrite the risk and achieve the company's mortality goals. They are not negotiable. They are seldom, if ever, waived or, for that matter, *waivable.*

Elective requirements, as their name implies, are requirements ordered at the discretion of the underwriter. They are ordered because some bit of information on the application or in the substance of an age/amount requirement needs to be investigated, clarified, amplified or reconciled.

Most elective requirements are essential and cannot be dispensed with. On the other hand, many turn out to be unnecessary. Most important, many are the direct result of the producer embracing the Theory A approach to underwriting!

When we perform underwriting audits, it is painfully apparent how many elective requirements turn out to be of no real help to the underwriter in his appraisal of the risk. One wonders how many of these, and we are talking countless thousands of requirements a month industrywide, could have been avoided in the first place if only the producer had adopted a different, basic approach to underwriting.

That approach we call Theory B.

In *Star Wars* parlance, Theory A represents "the dark side" and Theory B is personified by a Jedi knight who comes to rescue a beleaguered producer (whose new business is in purgatorial orbit around the underwriter's desk!).

The basic tenet of Theory B is that producers and underwriters have a common goal: issue the policy as fast as possible. The longer an application lies fallow, the less its chances are of culminating in an in-force, premium-paying (not to mention commission-triggering, referral-generating) instrument.

The importance of this is huge, now in the 21st century, as alternative insurance sales modalities (e.g., bancassurance, direct mail, telemarketing, retail outlet sales, site sales and internet sales) compete with our traditional distribution system. The cornerstone of these new ways of selling insurance is that they dramatically reduce the interval from the decision to purchase insurance to the delivery of the policy.

All lofty premises aside, why would the underwriter *really* care if the policy gets issued sooner rather than later? Because stagnant, long-pending underwriting files attract the attention of the bosses! They are "loose cannons" which, time and again, come back to haunt underwriters in two ways:

1. **They are vulnerable to being audited. Every underwriting manager has access to a computer generated list of long pending files held by each of his underwriters. These files are ripe for an autopsy! When dissected, they are a high risk and can prove hazardous to the underwriter's performance evaluation. Ask any underwriter—the fewer old files, the better!**

2. **They attract nasty letters from producers, general agents and proposed insureds alike. The letters always seen to go to the underwriter's boss, or to his boss' boss, or even higher up the corporate food chain. The higher the letters go, the more brouhaha they incite. All of which serves to focus potentially unflattering attention on the underwriter!**

Clearly, both the producer and the home office underwriter are well-served to keep long pending files to the bare minimum. You can have a dramatic impact on making this happen. All you have to do is two things:

1. **Renounce Theory A.**

2. **Embrace Theory B.**

Recognize that producers and home office underwriters share a common self-interest called expediting pending cases. Facilitate this by:

- *Fully* **asking and dutifully recording the full answers to all questions on the application.**

- **Writing cover letters whenever they can help amplify the application or expedite the underwriting process.**

It is as simple as this: Theory A creates delays, jeopardizes your business and, ultimately, fosters mistrust, even paranoia. Theory B expedites your business and enhances and maximizes relationships between producers and underwriters.

Renounce Theory A.

Embrace Theory B.

If you cannot bring yourself to do this, do not read this book any further. The Theory A mindset is incompatible with what lies ahead.

Agents' Statement Forms

Your personal knowledge of the applicant can be used to get the policy issued promptly and as applied for. Most insurers have an Agent's Statement or section of the application form that does not become part of the policy. It asks questions about the sale and permits you to share observations about the proposed insured and the purpose of the coverage. A well-completed Agent's Statement might reduce the need for cover letters for smaller amounts of coverage.

The "Purpose of Coverage" question often draws derisive comments from agents. When properly answered, though, it can minimize misunderstandings by underwriters and potential delays caused by additional requirements. For example, if the purpose of the insurance is to cover a business loan, say so. Do not simply leave the question blank or write "key person." As explained in Chapter 10, "Financial Underwriting: Does It Make Sense?", loan coverages are underwritten differently than pure key person insurance.

Asking Questions and Recording Answers

The three most important things to strive for when you complete applications are:

1. **accuracy;**

2. **clarity; and**

3. **thoroughness.**

Recording accurate answers requires you to listen carefully when the applicant responds to questions. To be a successful salesperson, you must be effective at this. A small error can have significant implications.

For instance, there are three new pharmaceuticals with *very* similar names: Celexa (citaloprim), Cerebyx (fosphenytoin) and Celebrex (celecoxib). Their uses, on the other hand, are very different.

Celexa is an antidepressant. Cerebyx is used for seziures. Celecoxib is given mainly for degenerative arthritis. Imagine the implications of confusing these names on an insurance application!

Clarity in recording the answers requires that you write them so an underwriter can understand them. This means more than good penmanship. Even if you use a computer application format, descriptions of symptoms and other details must be perfectly clear to avoid unnecessary delay. If the client actually says, "I was a little dizzy during a severe bout of the flu six months ago," but you only write "Dizziness – six months ago," the underwriter will need to determine the cause of the dizziness and may order an unnecessary and time-consuming attending physician statement.

Thoroughness requires that you do not edit the applicant's responses to the questions. In fact, thoroughness will usually work in your favor to expedite approval and issue by minimizing the need for requirements. If the client above had said, "I experienced some dizziness six months ago," you may be able to help the underwriter avoid an APS by asking the client what the doctor determined to be the cause. If the client responded, "He said I just had a severe case of the flu and after I got over it, there was no more dizziness," you should add those details to the response.

Each insurer establishes routine guidelines for APSs and other requirements based upon its own mortality and morbidity experience, its market, product lines, cost strategies and other factors. Yet accuracy, clarity and thoroughness when taking the application will go a long way toward minimizing delays.

Occupation and Duties

For life insurance, advances in occupational safety and health over the past four decades have helped reduce the mortality risks associated with many dangerous jobs. Even such a hazardous industry as mining has improved practices so much that worker safety is a top priority today despite the inherent dangers of underground work.

The occupation questions on life application forms often ask for "duties" of the insured. If the duties of an occupation make a difference in the premium rate and/or accidental death benefit (ADB) or disability (DW), the completion of the application is the point at which you can help your client obtain the most favorable premium if the facts warrant. Use the cover letter to expand upon the reasons your client deserves a more favorable classification and offer supporting evidence, if available. Do not wait until you receive an undeliverable policy to present your case.

Occupation guidelines in the underwriting manuals of insurers typically use a combination of flat, extra premiums along with ratings or declination for ADB and DW when an occupation warrants it. Many insurers publish their occupation guidelines for their agents so a rate and/or denial of benefits can be quoted at the time of the sale.

Owner / Beneficiary / Insurable Interest

The proper completion of the Ownership and Beneficiary sections of the application form is another time-saver. (This topic is described more fully in Chapter 10.) Nevertheless, always explain the relationship of the owner or beneficiary, either in the "Details" section or in a cover letter if the relationship is unusual in any way.

To illustrate, a beneficiary designation of "friend" might be unacceptable without an explanation of the insurable interest, especially if the friend is also named as an owner.[1] Moreover, friends or distant relatives may share in a debt or hold an asset together, thereby creating a financial interest that may qualify as insurable. Explain it. Do not assume that because you understand the transaction the rationale will be self-evident to an underwriter.[2]

Other Insurance Coverage In-Force and/or Pending

If the application asks about this topic it is because the insurer will evaluate the total line of insurance and compare it to the demonstrated need. You must itemize the coverages with other insurers in addition to the company the client is applying to and usually indicate where any ADB is part of the existing coverage, especially on large amounts. It is common for insurers to cap the acceptable level of ADB they will participate in, let alone issue on their own. Based upon large amount insurance mortality studies by the Society of Actuaries (conducted every six to eight years for the past sixty years), accidental death mortality rises as the amount of coverage rises, both with and without ADB. These deaths include vehicular, airplane and leisure activity accidents plus homicides and suicides.

Also, where in-force coverages had different purposes, owners and/or beneficiaries, a cover letter outlining those details will minimize requests for clarification from the underwriter. That is especially important for clients who purchase large amounts of coverage for multiple uses – personal, business, estate planning, charitable giving and so on.

When coverage is pending with another insurer, it should not only be listed but also explained.

- **Is this a competitive situation or will both policies be accepted?**
- **If both will be accepted, why is the coverage being split between insurers?**

Although the explanations might be perfectly logical, the underwriter must evaluate them on the basis of the total coverage that will be placed. The underwriter must also be satisfied that the concurrent purchase of insurance with different companies is not simply a maneuver to avoid underwriting requirements. The requirements will probably be necessary anyway based upon the combined amount.

Reporting the Proposed Insured's Medical History

Your client's medical history is recorded on what is universally referred to in North America as the Part II of the application. It consists of a series of medical questions, some of which are focused on a particular bodily system and a related group of impairments. Other questions are specific with regard to matters such as your client's last visit to a physician, the use of tobacco, etc.

Traditionally, these questions on the Part II are formally asked, and the answers officially recorded, by a producer, a paramedical technician or a physician.

Not long ago, the medical was dominant, the paramedical almost nonexistent and the non-medical reserved for smaller cases. Beginning in the 1970s and accelerating quickly during the next decade, the advantages of the paramedical (convenience, cost-effectiveness and a faster turnaround than an MD exam) became widely recognized. By the early 1980s, most of the business that had been designated for examination by a physician was now eligible for paramedical submission. Indeed, a producer might encounter a penalty for having a physician examine a case that falls within the paramedical limits!

Non-medical limits increased abruptly in the late 1970s. Today, a significant share of all life and disability applications are eligible for non-medical submission. In these cases, the producer takes on a very solemn accountability; *he* is the medical history taker.

The thoroughness with which the medical history questions are asked and the client's answers recorded will have a profound impact on the insurer's mortality/morbidity results and, hence, on its profitability. The producer's performance in the role of medical history taker may also have a direct impact on the length of his career. Careers have been ended abruptly in the wake of material and significant "oversights" in answers recorded on non-medicals.

Taking and Recording the Medical History

"The time to find out about a potential medical condition is not at the application stage but during the fact-finding part of the interview."[3]

–Bob Littell, CLU, ChFC
Broker's Resource Center, Inc.

An all-important rule of taking a medical history is that it should not be done for the *first time* during the completion of the application! Key medical questions should be asked for the first time during the fact finding interview.

The fact finder does more than guide the producer in making recommendations regarding the type of insurance, the amount of coverage, etc. It should also identify possible underwriting problems. Some producers go over the entire Part II during the fact finding interview. More often, a shorter list of key questions are asked regarding recent medical problems: tobacco, alcohol and drug use, current prescription and over-the-counter medications, etc. If "preferred/superpreferred" coverage is available, the parameters for qualifying are usually discussed.

Reviewing the medical history during the fact finding interview has three advantages:

1. **The producer's recommendations as to the plan of insurance, the expected premium, etc., can be adjusted in accordance with the uncovered medical facts.**

2. **The producer is alerted to possible insurability problems and can take steps to expedite the underwriting process.**

3. **In cases where adverse information is revealed, the groundwork can be laid for delivering a potentially rated policy.**

Five Essential Questions to Ask About Any Medical History

When the client gives a "Yes" response to a Part II question about a specific medical condition or illness, there are five essential questions that should be asked by you and answered by the client. If these questions are asked and the answers dutifully recorded, the net impact will be *fewer* requirements and *faster* underwriting approval of the case.

An example will help put the importance of this into perspective.

In 1973, as a trainee underwriter, I [HG] saw the following medical "history" written on a non-medical Part II of a life insurance application on a 25 year-old male. It is a classic example of how *not* to report a medical history!

"Colitis. OK now!"

Colitis means inflammation of the large intestine.

There are three, basic kinds of "colitis" one might see more than rarely in young adults:

1.   **Ulcerative colitis, which is sometimes rated and occasionally declined.**

2.   **Spastic or mucous colitis (also known as irritable bowel syndrome), which is seldom of concern in life underwriting but might have significant implications for disability insurance.**

3.   **The "green apple quick-step," an abrupt and definitive response to bowel hyperactivity that is typically induced by overindulgence and of no real interest to anyone (except the unfortunate individual experiencing it!).**

Which of these do you think is most likely to be the underlying cause of the proposed insured's "colitis"?

It is impossible to even make a calculated guess. Fact: a worthless medical history such as "Colitis. OK now!" provides no information of any value whatsoever to the underwriter. Other than knowing the client's medical problem was related to the function of his lower G.I. tract, the underwriter cannot begin to make inferences as to whether this is a potentially significant impairment (such as ulcerative colitis) or a matter of absolutely no underwriting significance at all (see point number 3 above).

Since "Colitis. OK now!" might be important, I asked for two requirements:

1.   **an attending physician's statement (APS); and**

2.   **a medical questionnaire.**

Instead of the case potentially being approved during the initial underwriting review, it was put into my pending file where, depending upon the attending physician's response time, it might have languished for a week, a month or (sadly), even longer.

Worse, the producer was forced into a non-selling, non-delivering encounter with his client in order to get the questionnaire completed. Nowadays, such a questionnaire might be completed by the home office personnel over the telephone, with the answers acknowledged and signed as a delivery requirement. Either way, the sale is placed in jeopardy. And the underwriting process keeps going on and on and on, just like that rabbit on the battery commercial!

Imagine if this client's medical history had been more thoroughly recorded on the Part II to read: "June, 1973. Episode of colitis after vacation in Cancun. Prescribed Lomotil by Emergency Room M.D. No recurrence."

Is this ulcerative colitis? No. Is this spastic/mucous colitis? No.

The use of the term "colitis" is actually unfortunate in this secnario. This was traveler's diarrhea, nothing more, as it turned out.

No APS was actually needed. Indeed, since he was seen by an emergency room doctor, there was probably no mention of the episode in his personal physician's records anyway. No medical questionnaire was truly necessary. All the needed information could *and should* have been provided on the Part II.

Approved as applied for on the initial review – *if the Part II had been properly completed.*

These are the five essential questions that should be asked about any medical history worthy of being reported on the Part II.

1. **What was the impairment? If you do not know the precise medical name, can you identify the bodily system involved and describe the symptom(s)?**

2. **When was it diagnosed? When were the first symptoms experienced? Month and year is adequate.**

3. **When was the last episode of symptoms? Again, month and year.**

4. **How was it treated? Be as *specific as possible*. Do not say "medication." Name the drug. Do not say "surgery." Name or describe the procedure.**

5. **Who was the physician seen for this?**

Identifying the impairment is extremely important. It might be the key to how the case is approached in underwriting.

Do not say "hepatitis." There are five major kinds of viral hepatitis alone, not to mention other forms related to defective immune system function, alcohol abuse, chronic obesity, medication reactions and so forth.

Ask your client which type of "hepatitis" he had. From the underwriter's perspective, there is a huge difference between hepatitis A versus hepatitis C versus autoimmune hepatitis.

Another common example is skin cancer. Basal cell carcinoma is the most frequent form of skin cancer in humans. It is almost never fatal and seldom even potentially disabling, even on a short term basis. The same can be said for garden-variety, sun-exposure-induced squamous cell (epidermoid) skin carcinoma.

On the other hand, a significant percentage of malignant melanomas of the skin metastasize and cause death.

If your client says he had a "skin cancer" removed, ask what kind it was. Most people tend to ask questions when physicians use the word "cancer." Chances are your client knows the answer on the day of your fact finding interview. Chances are that information will (largely) determine how the case is underwritten. Ask.

One episode of basal cell carcinoma three years ago might not even justify the request for a physician's report. Conversely, every case of known or suspected malignant melanoma will be fully underwritten (which means the underwriter must see the pathology report).

It is a basic tenet of medical underwriting that the longer an individual has remained free of symptoms from an illness, the more likely he is to be cured. Thus, it is essential that the underwriter be given this information on the Part II. When was the impairment first discovered/diagnosed? When was the last episode of symptoms?

Let's say you have two children – both are boys, age 12 – proposed for insurance. Both have a history of epilepsy, diagnosed on the same day. Both take the same medication. Identical mortality risks, right? Maybe. The key variable is, when was the last seizure? If one boy had his last seizure five weeks prior to the application date and the other boy has been seizure free for five years, expect two radically different underwriting outcomes.

The frequency of symptoms should also be noted. An asthmatic who has two episodes a year during hay fever season is a much better risk, all other things being equal, than one who has 25 attacks throughout the year.

The importance of the fourth question cannot be overstated. Each year we present an intensive, day-long seminar for underwriters and others on "Pharmacology and Underwriting." One of the concepts we hammer home with example after example is that knowing *precisely* how an individual was treated (what *specific* medication) can be a key to making an underwriting decision. This can be especially important in one of those inevitable cases where the attending physician drags his heels on a request for medical information...and the producer needs the case to qualify for the President's Club or the cruise to Alaska!

You have two prospective clients. Both are males, in their forties and are rising stars in their respective banks. Three years ago, each experienced an episode of chest discomfort, sufficient enough to send each one to his physician. Each man was referred to a cardiologist who performed an evaluation. As it turned out, both men saw the same cardiologist! Unfortunately, that cardiologist has since long departed to his new practice...in Nepal! Since this episode was one year prior to the application date, the details were of considerable importance to this risk. An inquiry with each attending physician revealed that neither doctor had seen his patient since the cardiologist referral. There was no report from the cardiologist in either file.

Now what?

The first man had a treadmill stress test and they told him it was normal. He was given diazepam hydrochloride (Valium) to take as needed.

The second man had a treadmill and a thallium scan. They told him he would be fine. He was given isosorbide dinitrate (Isordil) to take each day.

The first case was approved as applied for; the second case was not. The only important difference was the medication, about which an appropriate inference was made by the underwriter.

This same rule applies to surgery. Let's say two middle-aged clients had a surgical procedure performed on that slender conduit connecting the throat and the stomach which is known as the esophagus.

The first client had a partial esophagectomy, the second had a fundoplication. Is there a difference? You bet! A partial esophagectomy means cancer or a precancerous condition, until proven otherwise by a careful reading of the pathology report. Fundoplication, a procedure to treat inflammation and acid reflux, does not have the same dire underwriting implications.

A complete answer to question four is vital. Do not say "medication." Write down the name of the specific drug. Do not say "surgery." Write down the name of the procedure, or at least describe what was done.

Ask, then thoroughly record, the answers to the five essential questions every time you take your client's medical history. If you do this, three good things will happen to you:

1. **Fewer requirements will be ordered on your business by underwriters.**

2. **More cases will be approved – faster.**

3. **In the long run, you will have fewer adverse actions because:**

   - **fewer files will be closed; and**

   - **some seemingly unfavorable scenarios will be deemed insurable as a direct result of your completeness and attention to detail.**

The Tobacco Use Question

For almost two decades, virtually all North American life and disability carriers have made use of what is commonly called "smoker/nonsmoker" pricing. In the beginning, "smoker" status was reserved for those who smoked cigarettes within one year of the application date. Increasingly, "smoker" now includes cigarette, pipe, cigar and oral tobacco devotees, as well as individuals withdrawing from tobacco craving by using nicotine therapy (gum, patch, spray, etc.).

When actuary John M. Bragg, FSA, ACAS, MAAA, described smokers as "the biggest impaired risk group" he was not exaggerating. Cigarette smoking is the number one preventable cause of mortality and morbidity. It is (conservatively) linked to four tables of excess mortality risk.

One in four American adults smokes cigarettes, with the percentage of cigarette users stablizing in the mid-1990s after the steep, two decade decline. An additional 5 percent of Americans consume tobacco in some other form, in most cases incurring significant risk from their tobacco use proclivities.

I [HG] know a producer from Pittsburgh who is a weekend jogger, with an ideal build and a normal blood pressure level, who ate a balanced diet and had parents who lived into their eighties. He also smoked 2-5 cigarettes a day. Nobody is perfect!

When he applied for insurance, he rationalized that the insurer could not possibly see the length and breadth of his ideal risk profile. He objected to the fact that because he was, in his words, "a light smoker of low tar cigarettes," he would, nonetheless, be put into the same risk category as his father-in-law who smoked three packs of Camels a day. He decided to take matters into his own hands. He lied about his tobacco use on the Part II and the insurer discovered his deception some months later. He now sells shoes in Scranton.

It is important to ask and record the client's answer to the tobacco use question with the same thoroughness as every other application question. If you suspect your client may be giving a less-than-accurate answer (which, in the absence of psychosis, means he said, "No," when the *correct* answer was, "Yes"), you might want to suggest to him that if he misrepresents his tobacco use and succeeds in acquiring coverage at "non-smoker" rates, he will be at risk for redress by the insurer. The policy could be reformed (reissued at smoker rates) or rescinded altogether during the contestable period. Benefits payable under the policy could be contested on the grounds of material misrepresentation. Indeed, the benefits not only could be, but very likely will be, contested if the insured truly misrepresented his tobacco use practices.

Misrepresenting tobacco use practices when applying for life or disability insurance is Russian roulette; it is not worth the risk. Make sure your client understands that if you have any reason to think that his answers might be anything less than truthful.

Special Questionnaires and Forms

You can assist the underwriter in properly analyzing the risk associated with such activities as private aviation or avocations like scuba diving or motor vehicle racing by using the special supplemental questionnaires provided by many insurers. These forms might be required rather than voluntary and may even become part of the policy in some states. The forms ask questions about specific details of an activity that involves extra risk. Your attention to their careful completion can help avoid delays and assist the underwriter in making the distinctions between risk levels that determine insurability, premium and/or policy exclusions.

Scuba diving, for example, is evaluated on the basis of type of equipment used, diving locations, depth and frequency of dives, certification(s) received and other factors. In addition to the questionnaire, you might also benefit by submitting a copy of the applicant's certification documents. If the diver has been involved in any accidents or other adverse situations associated with diving, it is better to give the details to the underwriter when the application is submitted.

Discovery of such information as a result of an inspection or APS disclosure can affect the perception of an underwriter concerning the applicant's motivation and candor. These principles apply to other activities and avocations, too. Do not let the underwriter be surprised by any adverse risk information that you become aware of, even if the application and special forms do not specifically ask for it.

Other special supplemental forms sometimes used by insurers include foreign travel/residence, business beneficiary, chest pain, diabetes and so on. These forms allow you to elaborate on risk factors in much greater detail than is practical on routine application forms. Even when their use is voluntary, use these forms to expedite underwriting and to obtain the most favorable appraisal.

Chapter Notes

1. In California, to the contrary, insurers must now allow "friend" as a beneficiary without restriction when the insured is the owner.
2. Ibid.
3. "Smoothing the Interview Stage With Impaired Risks," Bob Littell, *National Underwriter*, Life & Health/Financial Services Edition, December 4, 1995, page 12.
4. "Smokers: The Biggest Impaired Risk Group," John M. Bragg, *National Underwriter*, Life & Health/Financial Services Edition, November 16, 1998, page 8.

CHAPTER 4

Orchestrating Medical Requirements (No Excuses)

Preparing the Client for Examination and Medical Testing

If your client is required to have a paramedical exam, a full medical examination and/or any type of medical testing, there are a number of things you can do to prepare him. The main impact of the following preparatory interventions is to minimize the risk of adverse findings that could jeopardize the case.

There are two kinds of exam findings leading to abnormal test results:

1. **those due to an underlying medical condition or illness; and**

2. **those provoked by transient, unimportant, non-illness related causes. This latter finding is sometimes correctly called "false positive" findings.**

Even the most meticulous preparations cannot completely eliminate false positives. However, the likelihood of these gremlins compromising your client's insurability can be greatly reduced if we understand how certain factors may exert an adverse impact and then intervene to minimize the risk.

For example, both blood pressure and pulse readings can be raised by widely-consumed stimulants such as caffeine and nicotine.

A blood pressure reading consists of two numbers: the higher number is the systolic and the lower number is the diastolic. Medical research has shown that acute caffeine intake can hike systolic blood pressure by as much as 10 units. [Blood pressure is expressed in millimeters of mercury (mm Hg) as measured on the blood pressure recording device known as a sphygmomanometer.] The diastolic (lower) reading can go up by 8 units or more. This effect is experienced, according to one British study, for up to two hours after drinking caffeinated coffee (and probably other caffeinated beverages, such as teas and colas, as well).

Cigarette smoking can similarly increase blood pressure. The above mentioned British study showed that the effects of smoking did not last quite as long as those induced by caffaine. Yet, they can potentially raise both systolic and diastolic blood pressure for an interval of time after smoking (or, for that matter, chewing).

Nicotine and caffeine taken together – as they often are – have been shown to have a synergistically adverse effect. In an Italian research report, the impact of both smoking and coffee drinking temporarily raised systolic blood pressure by as much as 12 units in female subjects!

Stress and recent alcohol intake can also influence blood pressure and pulse readings. Therefore, the following precuations should be taken in preparation before a paramedical or MD examination:

- **Your client should have a good night's sleep before the examination.**

- **Excessive caffeinated beverages (coffee, tea, some soft drinks) should be avoided for two hours prior to the exam.**

- **Tobacco should never be used within two hours of an exam. Not in any form. Ever.**

- **Alcoholic beverages should be shunned for eight hours or longer.**

Three additional factors have been shown to adversely affect blood pressure readings:

1. **Distended bladder. Make sure your client voids his urine specimen before his blood pressure is taken!**

2. **Narrow blood pressure cuff. If your client has a large arm, whether muscular or obese, remind the examiner to use a wide arm cuff when taking his blood pressure.**

3. **The phenomenon known as "white coat hypertension."
    Loosely translated – medical authority figures in working
    garb (hence, "white coat") make some people tense. This can
    cause systolic blood pressure, in particular, to skyrocket when
    recorded in a clinical-like setting. Studies have shown that is
    twice as likely to happen if the person taking the blood
    pressure reading is a male MD as compared to a female nurse
    or technician.**

The solution: *Never submit a paramedically eleigible case with a MD
examination!* Use paramedicals whenever they are allowed.

A report from the University of Toronto Medical School published in the
Journal of American Medical Association (1995) reviewed all the factors thought
to affect the accuracy of blood pressure readings. The author listed two factors
under the heading "No Effect on BP" which should be noted from an
underwriting perspective.

1. **Chronic caffeine ingestion. Even though excess caffeine must
    be scrupulously avoided *within two hours of the exam*, regular
    use of caffeinated beverages does not produce chronically
    elevated blood pressure.**

2. **Decongestant nasal sprays. Millions of Americans use nasal
    decongestants that contain adrenalin-like chemicals. It seems
    logical to infer that recent use of these preparations could
    raise one's blood pressure. Not true.**

In preparing your client for laboratory testing, attention must be focused on
four factors:

1. **No blood or urine specimens should be collected *less than* 120
    minutes after the last intake of food. Notice I said 120
    minutes, not two hours. Do not be imprecise! There may not
    be much difference in your mind between 90 minutes and
    two hours; there is, however, a *dramatic difference* between
    these two time intervals in terms of glucose metabolism
    following food ingestion. Also, it should not be necessary to
    add that your client's last meal prior to blood and urine
    specimen collection should not be a feeding frenzy in a
    doughnut shop!**

2. **Avoid strenuous exercise for at least 12 hours prior to the
    exam for three important reasons.**

    i) **First, a liver enzyme known as AST (SGOT), which is a
        part of every full blood profile, is susceptible to**

temporary elevation from muscle trauma from vigorous exercise.

ii) Second, both protein (albumin) and blood (red blood cells, hematuria) have been known to show up in urine specimens as a result of recent exercise.

iii) Third, a 1996 research study published in *Clinical Chemistry* journal revealed that stationary bicycling can raise a male's prostate specific antigen (PSA) level as much as three-fold. That could lead to additional testing or even outright declination of the risk.

3. Insurance blood and urine tests should, ideally, be avoided after a recent trauma or physical injury (e.g., a car accident or a broken bone), in the presence of a fever or during an acute respiratory infection (or any other acute illness) or in the first few days after any inpatient hospitalization. In most cases, these scenarios probably will not have any detrimental effects whatsoever on lab test results. But why take the chance when these situations can almost always be easily avoided in proximity to blood and urine testing?

4. Make sure that you question your client thoroughly about any use of prescription and over-the-counter medicines and related remedies. As stated earlier, this includes herbs, hormones, dietary supplements taken for whatever reason and so on. The American Association for Clinical Chemistry (the professional association of pathologists who set the standards for lab tests) publishes an 800 page reference book entitled, *Effects of Drugs on Clinical Laboratory Tests*. Any questions?

Some years ago, this underwriter [HG] saw a case which made the importance of knowing about medication crystal clear to me. The proposed insured was a 28 year-old accountant from Toronto. His only medical history was that he had experienced two epileptic seizures more than a decade before; the prospect also stated that he had been seizure-free since the second episode. Careful evaluation by a neurologist had proven negative for a serious underlying cause.

The only other adversity on this case happened to be an elevation of the GGT liver enzyme. It reported out at 360 units (normal range = 0-65 units) on the mandatory screening full blood profile.

A GGT elevation of that magnitude is incompatible with approving a life insurance application, at least until after further tests are performed to try to ascertain the potential significance of this finding. At the time this case was underwritten, such tests (first and foremost, the alcohol marker HAA; see Chapter 5) were not available to underwriters. Thus, this case was declined.

Arrangements were made to get the insurance lab test results to the insured's personal physician. Then, the proposed insured went to see that physician, concerned that his elevated GGT was a sign of a serious illness.

The physician, of course, knew right away what was happening so he reassured his patient and then wrote a (pointed) letter to this underwriter. In that letter the physician explained that his patient was taking the antiseizure drug Dilantin as a precaution against any further seizures. The MD corrrectly pointed out that this medication is one of several which often raise the GGT, sometimes as much as *ten times the normal limit!* Furthermore, the mechanism underlying this GGT elevation is completely harmless and should not, in truth, compromise his patient's insurability in any way.

Why, then, did this underwriter decline the case? *Because I did not know that the insured was taking this medication!* That fact was not disclosed anywhere on the Part II. The producer did not ask this client, specifically, about the use of medication. Needless to add, there was no cover letter.

Application declined. Sale lost. Client scared. MD irritated. Nobody won!

The only way an underwriter can make the connection between an abnormal lab test result and the fact that your client uses a medication capable of causing that abnormality is *if the underwriter knows your client is taking that medication!* Make sure the use of medications (once again, include such things as herbs, hormones and dietary supplements taken for whatever reason) is addressed and resolved on every case you submit.

Choosing and Working With Paramedical Examiners, Physician Examiners and Special Testing Facilities

Most insurers appoint a number of paramedical firms to perform insurance exams as well as blood, urine and oral fluid specimen collections. Then, the insurers empower the producer to select which of the approved firms will be utilized on any given case. The same is usually true for MD examiners. The insurer may have a roster of eligible physicians but it leaves the choice of the actual examiner to the producer.

If we were producers, we would insist on four things from an examiner:

1. **A client-friendly atmosphere with professional attire and courteous, professional conduct.**

2. **A sense of urgency which means that appointments are kept promptly. Delays are lost sales waiting to happen.**

3. **Proper technique in lab specimen collection and prompt forwarding of those specimens to the designated testing laboratory.**

4. **Attentively asking the medical questions and then carefully recording the client's entire answers in such a way that it will facilitate the underwriter's review of the file.**

Regarding the collection and submission of lab specimens, there are two clues that indicate a problem might exist with the examiner:

1. **More than an occasional home office request for a repeat specimen using such pretexts as QNS (quantity not sufficient) or hemolysis (the blood specimen was not properly handled prior to shipment to the lab).**

2. **Delays in getting the test results reported by the testing lab to the insurer. Laboratories pride themselves on the speedy reporting of test results to insurers. (Indeed, this is one way in which they compete for business!) Given that most results are reported via computer, if the test reports on your business consistently trickle in, the problem may lie with delayed shipments and other handling problems attributable to the examiner.**

Paramedical exams (in some cases, physician exams) may be mobile (performed on your client's premises) or conducted at fixed site testing centers. There are pros and cons to both. Mobile exams tend to be more convenient while fixed site exam centers offer the advantage of special testing facilities that are diffuclt or impossible to do on a mobile basis.

In general, there is little advantage to ruminating over the choice of the physician for a full medical exam. Some companies discourage using the client's personal physician while others are ambivalent on this point.

There is, in our view, only one *essential* rule to be adhered to when selecting an MD examiner: if your client has a history of a heart murmur or some other heart condition, make sure the examiner is an internist or, even better, a cardiologist. Follow company rules, of course, but try to avoid having your client sent back for a second opinion simply because the original exam was done by a less qualified individual!

The other criterion worth considering when selecting a medical examiner is the availability of testing facilities for such things as treadmill stress tests and pulmonary function tests. If the medical examiner cannot perform those tests in his office, does he have convenient access to facilities where they can be done, without excessive delays, inconvenience to your client or objectionably high fees?

The Attending Physician's Statement

Whether you call them attending physicians' statements (APSs) as we do in North America, attending physicians' reports (APRs) or physicians' medical reports (PMRs) as they do in other countries, the fact is that reports from physicians (and clinics and hospitals) detailing the clients' medical histories are essential sources of underwriting information.

If you do not believe this, try to get one waived!

The APS comes in many shapes and sizes. We have seen reports ranging from one sentence (a "very busy" Long Island psychiatrist) to 200 hundred pages (the U.S. military records on a master sergeant with 30 years of active duty and a fondness for spirits!).

Some physicians send photocopies of their records, others dictate a narrative report which their secretaries neatly transcribe on their letterhead. Occasionally, a physician will actually fill out the APS form sent by the insurer.

Today, a significant portion of APS reports are gathered for insurers by service firms that promise to speed up collection for a fee. Since APS reports are the slowest requirements (typically, the *last* piece of information to arrive on any pending case), insurers gladly pay such fees to expedite the APS process. Reports are also mailed or faxed directly from physicians to insurers; some are picked up and conveyed by zealous producers.

APS Realities and the Producer

It's important to recognize how the attending physician's report and the agent interact.

- **Why are there sometimes three, four or even five APS reports required on one case? Because the client often sees multiple physicians. The personal physician (report #1) sends the client to a specialist (report #2) who hospitalizes him for a workup (report #3) and calls in a subspecialist to consult (report #4) and a surgeon to perform a biopsy (report #5). All of those reports might involve just one impairment. What if there are two?**

- **Sometimes (but not as often as you would like), the report from the personal physician contains details, maybe even actual copies, of correspondence from specialists, of discharge summaries from hospitals, of pathology reports, etc. Those may allow the underwriter to waive other outstanding APSs and take faster action. Most of the time, however, the case remains pending until all APSs are received and reviewed.**

- **Avoid doing business with hypochondriacs unless you are a very patient person.**

- **Shorter is not better! Very terse medical reports often raise as many questions as they answer. They may force the underwriter to *write back* for amplification or to order additional tests. In either scenario, the case is surely delayed and might be jeopardized further. Contrary to popular belief, you and your client are not well served when physicians greatly abbreviate or overly edit their reports to life insurers!**

- **Depending upon the nature of the history, certain pieces of information might be vital. The classic example is the cancer pathology report. You cannot underwrite a cancer risk without knowing *precisely* which kind of cancer (there are hundreds) the client had. You cannot ascertain insurability in anyone with a history of cancer until you examine, in detail, the specifics of the pathology report as to extent of disease, prognostic factors, etc.**

- **Another example of a *vital* underwriting document is the full report from a cardiac catheterization that will contain all-important measurements that distinguish healthy hearts from transplant candidates.**

If you are involved in expediting the APS, be alert to the need for these essential documents. Remember, if the APS on a cancer case is sent in without a copy of the pathology report, the case file goes back into orbit around the underwriter's desk while a second request gets sent to the physician. Delays mean lost sales, especially on cancer survivors who often approach insurance acquisition apprehensively.

APS Reports are Confidential

The contents of APS reports are totally confidential. The proposed insured has authorized his physician to release records *to the insurance company* for the express purpose of obtaining approval of his application for insurance. The client and the physician have an expectation that this information will be treated as *utterly* confidential.

Out of respect for the confidentiality of patient records, underwriters are not at liberty to discuss the contents of APS reports with producers. Each insurer has, in place, a step-by-step feedback loop which allows adverse medical information to get back to the client. This feedback loop should be used when it is needed.

How Can Producers Expedite the APS?

- **Make sure the medical history is recorded as accurately as possible. Mistakes, omissions, anything that delays the ordering of essential reports slows down the underwriting process. The vast majority of the long-pending cases closed for "information called for" involve outstanding APSs.**

- **Provide as much information as possible about the physicians who were consulted. Do not write "Dr. Jones in New York City." Instead, indicate Philip T. Jones, M.D. 12345 Park Avenue, New York, NY. Sales have been lost because a request for an APS was sent to the *wrong* Dr. Jones!**

- **Make sure you have a properly signed authorization. If you do not, the whole APS gathering process is placed on hold until one is obtained.**

- **If company rules permit, order the APSs directly from your agency. The sooner the report is ordered, the sooner it arrives. Anything you can do to expedite the release of medical records to the insurer, *so long as confidentiality is never compromised*, will have the ultimate impact of increasing case approvals.**

The APS Report Cannot Be Obtained–Now What?

If a physician balks at complying with the client's authorization to send a report, the client should remind him that those records are the property of the patient, not the doctor! In the final analysis, the client, as the patient, is not *asking* the physician or hospital to send a report of his records, he is *telling* them to do so. We do not couch things so bluntly, but that is the reality of the situation.

If the APS is ultimately inaccessible, the underwriter will ask himself these questions:

- **Is there an alternative source for this information? How about a second physician who might have some correspondence related to this history? Is there a copy of the hospital discharge summary in the file of the physician who was called to consult on the case?**

- **Might current testing provide enough information in order to take action in lieu of the APS? Is the cost of such testing within the limits of the underwriting budget? Must the application be postponed until the client, at his own expense, obtains the necessary tests? The key question is, What is the medical history? A heart murmur might be reconciled with a cardiologist's examination or an echocardiogram. A complex neurological history cannot be underwritten without the APS.**

- **Can action be taken without the APS? An expanded statement from the client with as many details as he can remember will be essential if this option is to be seriously entertained. Another possibility is a telephone interview (a personal history interview) with the prospect. Action may then be taken with the clear understanding that it is for "this amount of coverage only" and that additional insurance will require further underwriting. Realistically, taking action with key information missing often results in a more conservative underwriting decision.**

CHAPTER 5

Understanding and Explaining Medical Tests

Lab Testing in Underwriting

Although tests performed on blood and urine specimens collected from proposed insureds have been utilized in risk selection for decades, it was not until the mid-1980s that these tests became a prominent part of life underwriting. This occured for two reasons.

1. **The AIDS pandemic raised concerns for a potentially huge mortality and morbidity impact. The only way to observe for infection with the HIV virus is to test.**

2. **The second reason for the ascendancy of lab tests as underwriting tools is their cost effectiveness as compared to traditional tools. A number of published protective value studies have proven that lab tests provide more "bang for the buck" than other medical tests. They are also much more convenient to perform as well as less time-consuming than such things as electrocardiograms and chest x-rays.**

The vast majority of testing for underwriting purposes involves three entities:

1. **automated, multi-component blood tests, referred to simply as "full blood profiles";**

2. **urine specimens tested both for typical ingredients (protein and sugar) and for special components such as cotinine ("nicotine") and drugs of abuse; and**

3. **oral fluid (saliva) profiles.**

Both urine and oral fluid testing have come to play growing roles in life, health and disability underwriting. The U.S. Food and Drug Administration has now fully approved urine-based and oral fluid-based HIV tests, prompting many insurers to make wider use of those alternatives to blood tests, mainly at younger ages (up to age 40 or, perhaps, age 45) and for smaller amounts of coverage.

This chapter will examine the principle components of blood, urine and oral fluid tests as they are used in risk selection.

Medical testing is a routine part of life insurance and disability income insurance underwriting. Such tests may be required in three distinct contexts:

1. **as age/amount requirements, based upon the age of the proposed insured and/or the amount of coverage applied for (currently, or cumulatively over some stated interval of time);**

2. **selectively ordered by the underwriter based upon the medical history recorded on the Part II or on facts disclosed on the attending physician's statement, inspection report, personal history interview or even the motor vehicle report; or**

3. **as a recheck of a test that was previously requested, received and analyzed. This occurs primarily with blood pressure readings and urine specimens.**

In most cases, the agent is responsible for making the arrangements to have the test completed. This also means the agent has some impact on how the test is performed. That impact can be vital when it comes to minimizing the chance of a false positive test.

Blood Tests

The dominant format for blood testing in insurance is a multi-component blood chemistry profile similar to those used in clinical medicine. Often, however, there are some important differences as to which tests are included.

Screening the full blood profile typically contains between 15 and 20 individual components. In addition, so-called "reflex tests" may be requested by the underwriter. Reflex tests may be sought because of some aspect of the proposed insured's medical history or because of an abnormality detected on one of the routine tests.

In many cases, insurers will give instructions to testing laboratories to immediately perform specific reflex tests when analysis of the routine tests shows a specific abnormality (for example, performing the alcohol marker test known as HAA when the GGT liver enzyme test is elevated). At other times, a reflex test will be ordered by the underwriter after he sees the results of the screening blood profile or reviews an APS.

Insurance labs also offer abbreviated blood test profiles consisting of fewer components than a full profile. These may be variously labeled as "mini" or "micro" profiles. The components may be customized by the laboratory to accommodate the specific requests of the insurance company's chief underwriter. The two test components most likely to be included on any abbreviated blood profile are the HIV (AIDS) test and the GGT test.

Traditionally, tests are performed on blood specimens collected by forearm venipuncture. This is the way in which most blood specimens are collected for clinical use as well. These specimens, in liquid form, are then centrifuged ("spun down") by the paramedical technician and shipped off to the insurance laboratory for analysis.

With the rapid increase in blood testing in insurance in the 1980s, a novel collection technique involving the use of specially treated filter paper was introduced into insurance testing. Known as the dried blood spot (DBS), this technique is used on many of the blood specimens collected by the fingerstick blood drawing method. Since the amount of blood collected for a DBS is quite small, the resulting profile is typically limited to a few test components. There is apt to be a higher incidence of repeated testing as well because the first specimen comes back labeled QNS ("quantity not sufficient") or SUFA ("specimen unsuitable for analysis").

Anytime one screens a large population of, ostensibly, well individuals with a battery of medical tests, there will be some false positive results. A test is deemed "false positive" if it is abnormal ("positive") in an individual who does not actually have the impairment(s) for which the test is intended as a screen.

The producer may minimize the risk of false positive tests on his clients by advising them to take precautions prior to testing. Simply stated, these important precautions are:

- **Do not have the blood drawn within two hours of food intake. Furthermore, make sure the last meal was not a bag of chocolate chip cookies!**

- Ask the client to avoid vigorous physical exercise on the same day as the blood drawing. Muscle trauma from strenuous exercise might affect the test components. Occasionally, this may be significant enough to result in adverse underwriting action especially with regard to the liver enzyme AST (SGOT) and, possibly, the prostate specific antigen (PSA).

- Do not have the blood specimens collected when the insured has a fever or acute infection, shortly after an accident or other physical trauma, or until several days have elapsed after hospitalization for any reason.

The final "rule of thumb" relates to information the agent wants the underwriter to have at the time the underwriter reviews the blood profile. Specifically, the underwriter needs to know if the insured is taking any medication or equivalent. This includes prescription drugs, over-the-counter pharmaceuticals, herbal remedies, large doses of dietary or body building supplements, hormone replacement therapy, oral contraceptives, etc.

It is an understatement to say that medications as well as various "alternative medicine" remedies can provoke abnormalities affecting key blood profile test components. More to the point, such abnormalities are (almost) always both temporary and free of symptoms. *The underwriter must always be told of all medications and related remedies taken by the proposed insured.* To fail to question your client thoroughly on this point is to play Russian roulette!

HIV (AIDS) Testing

The test for infection with the AIDS virus is the HIV-1 test. There are actually two distinct viruses which result in AIDS: HIV-1 and HIV-2. Virtually all North American cases of AIDS are related to HIV-1. Therefore, we will refer to the AIDS test simply as the HIV test.

The HIV test consists of two components:

1. a screening test, which is inexpensive and easy to perform; and

2. a confirmatory test which is more expensive and more difficult to perform and, as its name implies, is used to confirm screening test findings. In HIV testing, the screening test is an ELISA (enzyme-linked immunosorbent assay) test and the confirmatory test is a western blot test.

Please note: "ELISA" and "western blot" refer only to test methodologies, not to tests done solely and exclusively for HIV. In other words, if an individual has had an ELISA test, we know the methodology by which he was tested. We do not know, based upon that information alone, that he was tested specifically for AIDS. That would be confirmed only if he was said to have had, specifically, an "HIV-1 ELISA" test rather than simply an "ELISA" test. The same is true for a western blot testing procedure.

If an insurance applicant has a *repeatedly* positive HIV ELISA test, the same blood specimen is then analyzed with the western blot (confirmatory) test. If the western blot HIV test is negative (normal), the individual is not infected with the HIV virus and the ELISA test was a false positive.

False positive ELISA tests are uncommon but still many times more common than true positive ELISA tests. This has no impact on the applicant, however, because no adverse information is reported to the insurance company so long as the western blot turns out negative (normal).

If the western blot test is positive, based upon the strict criteria adhered to in making that determination, the individual is deemed to be infected with the HIV virus.

There is a third scenario which might arise in what is known as an "indeterminate" western blot test. The test does not meet the rigorous criteria set for a positive test; on the other hand, it is not completely normal, either. It shows findings in what one might call a "gray zone."

The analysis of an indeterminate western blot test takes into account many factors. Some indeterminate tests might be able to be disregarded while others might require postponement or further testing.

As mentioned earlier, HIV screening and confirmation testing is now routinely done on both urine and oral fluid specimens. The same ground rules apply to these tests.

HIV test results, like all lab test results used in underwriting, are handled with extreme attention to both chain of custody and confidentiality. The former refers to techniques used to assure that the specimen being tested is, in fact, the same specimen taken from the proposed insured. Chain of custody procedures are rigorous, involving bar codes, multiple signatures and meticulous handling procedures by the examiners and in the laboratories.

Confidentiality of test results is equally important. One of the reasons producers are sometimes frustrated by rules and regulations that appear to obstruct the sales process is that insurers place the highest priority on maintaining strict confidentiality with regard to test results. This is true not only for AIDS tests but for all tests. Typically, the release of lab test information to interested parties, including the insured's physician, will involve what seems, at first, to be an excessively bureaucratic procedure. That is to protect the client and to assure the strict confidentiality of this sensitive information. Abide by the rules—they serve you and your client well.

Blood Lipids

There are a number of tests, known collectively as blood lipids, which are routinely screened for in both insurance and clinical medicine. On the full blood profile, one is apt to find total cholesterol, HDL-cholesterol (HDL-C), LDL-cholesterol (LDL-C) and triglycerides.

Total cholesterol is probably the best known test related to the risk of developing coronary artery disease. Indeed, elevated blood cholesterol is one of the three cardinal risk factors for a heart attack, along with hypertension (high blood pressure) and cigarette smoking.

In reality, total cholesterol is a fairly insensitive screening test. Only a small percentage of individuals with coronary artery disease will have a significantly (from the underwriter's perspective) elevated total cholesterol. Thus, cholesterol readings are analyzed in conjunction with the other lipid components, particularly the HDL-C.

At the risk of oversimplification, it could be said that one's total cholesterol consists mainly of two major components: "good" cholesterol and "bad" cholesterol. The "good" cholesterol is the high density lipoprotein (HDL-C) fraction. It is felt to be "good" because it has been shown to be associated with getting excess "bad" cholesterol out of the arteries. Most studies have shown that, the higher your HDL-C , the lower your risk of a heart attack.

HDL-C is included in nearly all full blood profiles used in underwriting. When it is present, the underwriter will pay particular attention to the ratio of the total cholesterol to the HDL-C fraction. This is referred to as the TC:HDL-C ratio. The higher the ratio, the worse the risk...and vice versa. There are two caveats, though. Low total cholesterol, high HDL-C and favorable (that is to say, low) TC:HDL-C ratios play a key role in qualifying for "preferred risk" status.

Caveat #1: Extremely low cholesterol (less than 140 mg/dL), especially in longtime, heavy smokers and persons who have had a recent, unexplained/involuntary weight loss, might be seen by the underwriter as unfavorable. This is very appropriate but also very uncommon.

Caveat #2: Some persons with very high HDL-C also abuse alcohol. Heavy alcohol intake raises HDL-C. In one Scandinavian study, subjects with very high HDL-C had a greatly increased incidence of alcohol-related mortality, especially from accidents. Therefore, when HDL-C is unusually high, the underwriter may require an alcohol marker test [discussed later in this chapter].

The LDL-cholesterol (LDL-C) test measures the "bad" portion of cholesterol, that is, the portion associated with an increased risk of coronary artery disease. Significantly elevated LDL-C may be used in conjunction with elevated total cholesterol and with low HDL-C to conclude that one's lipid profile is unfavorable for underwriting purposes.

The triglycerides test is also part of the blood lipid aspect of the full blood profile. Elevated triglycerides levels are consistently shown, in study after study, to be linked to an increased risk of circulatory disease, especially coronary artery disease. High triglycerides readings are also often seen with diabetes. Finally, individuals with extremely elevated triglycerides levels may suffer from a disorder which can adversely affect their pancreas or bile ducts.

One of the reasons for requiring that blood specimens are not collected within two hours of eating is that blood triglyceride levels are exquisitely sensitive to recent carbohydrate ingestion. Frequently, instruction will be given for a 12-14 hour fast. In reality, however, it is unusual for individuals who have not consumed carbohydrates in any significant quantity within two hours of the blood drawing to have triglyceride levels high enough to compromise insurability. That is, of course, unless they have an underlying impairment!

In our judgement, fasting longer than two hours before a blood specimen is collected has little, if any, importance in insurance testing. On the other hand, the 120-minute fast is essential. Anything less, to use the language of the fisherman, is like trolling…for unnecessary ratings!

The apolipoprotein test is a reflex test used occasionally to further assess the significance of elevated screening blood lipids. There are two components that are measured for underwriting purposes which are designated APO A-1 and APO B. APO A-1 is associated with HDL-cholesterol and might be called the "good" apolipoprotein. The reverse is true for APO B which is linked to LDL-C and, thus, to an increased risk of heart disease.

Blood Sugar and Diabetes

There are three types of diabetes mellitus:

1. **Type 1, which often begins in childhood or young adulthood and always requires insulin therapy;**

2. **Type 2, which is more apt to begin in mid-life or later and can often be treated with oral medications rather than insulin injections; and**

3. **Gestational, that is, occurring during pregnancy.**

These specific disorders are discussed in Chapter 6. The basic screening test for all three types of diabetes mellitus is the glucose (blood sugar) test.

Blood glucose levels are directly impacted by food intake. If glucose stood alone as the only test for diabetes, failure to surveillance the timing of the blood draw could result in many clients being rated or postponed. However, this risk is greatly diminished by the presence of the fructosamine test on insurance blood profiles.

Glucose in the bloodstream has an affinity for attaching to proteins, a process called glycosylation. The fructosamine test measures the level of glycosylated proteins. The results of this test are not altered significantly if the specimen was collected within two hours of the subject's last meal.

If the proposed insured has no history of diabetes but his screening blood glucose level shows a mild-to-moderate (generally, up to 200 mg/dL) elevation, the fructosamine test should settle the matter. If it is normal, the elevated glucose is assumed to be due to recent food intake. If the fructosamine is elevated, however, then the probability of diabetes (or a pre-diabetic condition) being present is greatly increased.

The final arbiter is the glycosylated hemoglobin test. This widely-used reflex test may also be referred to as glycohemoglobin or hemoglobin A-1c (Hb A-1c). It is similar to fructosamine in that it detects protein glycosylation. Yet, it measures glucose bound to just one protein— hemoglobin—the protein which, among other things, gives blood its dtsinctive coloration.

The glycosylated hemoglobin test is often ordered when fructosamine is mildly elevated. If both fructosamine and glycosylated hemoglobin are elevated, diabetes must be assumed to be present. However, if fructosamine is elevated and glycosylated hemoglobin is normal, the likelihood of diabetes is greatly decreased.

The glycosylated hemoglobin test is also the test of choice to evaluate a diabetic applicant to determine if he is experiencing adquate control of his blood sugar level. This, as you will read in the next chapter, is a major aspect of determining the insurability of a diabetic.

Kidney Function Tests

There are two kidney function tests on the insurance blood profile:

1. **BUN and creatinine.**

2. **BUN (blood urea nitrogen) measures by-products of protein metabolism in the blood. If the BUN is significantly elevated, kidney impairment is the likely explanation. Minimal elevations, however, might be caused by dehydration, antihypertensive medications, etc.**

Except in the elderly, creatinine is the superior screening test for kidney impairment. When blood creatinine levels are even mildly elevated, especially in the presence of high blood pressure, diabetes or a history of kidney impairment, the probability of kidney damage is greatly increased.

Whenever kidney impairment is suspected, based upon abnormalities of the BUN and/or creatinine, the underwriter also looks carefully at the urinalysis. The vast majority of individuals with malfunctioning kidneys will have one or more telltale urinary abnormalities. This includes protein (proteinuria, microalbuminuria), red blood cells (hematuria) and/or casts (cylindruria) in the urine.

Serum Proteins

There are three tests on the screening blood profile which measure levels of blood proteins:

1. **total protein;**

2. **albumin; and**

3. **globulin.**

Total protein, as the name implies, is the sum of all circulating proteins. It is rarely abnornal. The most disconcerting abnormality would be a higher than normal level in a geriatric applicant.

The most prevalent of the body's individual proteins is albumin. When an individual has lost a significant portion of his liver function, the blood albumin level will, eventually, fall. Thus, a blood albumin test with a result less than the lower limit of the stipulated normal range will always be considered significantly adverse by underwriters.

The third component is the globulin test. This is the sum of several subtypes of the protein known as globulin. Both elevations and below normal levels may be significant in underwriting, depending upon the medical history and other findings. Fortunately, abnormalities of all of these serum proteins are distinctly uncommon in insurance testing.

Liver Function Tests

There are five "liver function" tests on the insurance full blood profile. In fact, not one of them is *solely* reflective of liver disease, rather, there are many potential causes for elevations of some of these tests. On the other hand, an individual with *multiple* abnormal liver function tests has a high probability of having a significant liver impairment.

Four of the tests are liver enzymes; the one that is not an enzyme is bilirubin. Bilirubin is a byproduct of the breakdown and recycling of old red blood cells. It is made water soluble by the liver so it can be excreted from the body.

An elevated bilirubin (hyperbilirubinemia) might be seen in almost any liver disorder. If the bilirubin is high enough, the individual will be jaundiced (icteric), which means there will be a yellowish tinge to his skin, eyes, etc. Most underwriters concur that it is best that the jaundice be fully investigated, clinically, to establish its cause *before* insurance is issued.

There is a condition known as Gilbert's disease which happens to be the number one cause of isolated, mild-to-moderate elevations of the bilirubin in otherwise healthy individuals. Persons with this "impairment" should *always* have normal liver enzymes, etc. In fact, any coexisting elevation of a liver enzyme in someone with a raised bilirubin argues against Gilbert's disease being the cause of the high bilirubin reading.

Gilbert's disease is thought to be a relatively common, inherited condition. Most persons who have it will only experience high bilirubin and, in some cases, transient juandice after a period of sustained fasting. (Relax, a 120 minute mini-fast for insurance testing is not long enough to cause bilirubin to rise from this condition!) The main point, from an underwriting perspective, is that Gilbert's disease confers no mortality or significant morbidity risk.

The enzyme alkaline phosphatase (AP) will often elevate in individuals with liver disorders, particularly if the illness affects the liver's duct system. Since this often happens when liver diseases progress, any elevation of AP thought to be of liver origin is highly significant in underwriting.

On the other hand, AP is also prone to rise in many conditions affecting the bones. This includes fractures. Most bone disorders have little or no mortality significance. They might, however, have considerable morbidity impact.

The importance of an elevation of alkaline phosphatase is always determined by several factors, including the degree of elevation, the age of the individual, the medical history and, above all, whether or not there are coexisting abnormalities in other liver function tests and/or serum proteins.

The transaminase, or aminotransferase, enzymes AST and ALT are the most widely-used liver-related screening tests in medicine. In the past, they went by the names SGOT (AST) and SGPT (ALT) respectively. Those names are, unfortunately, still occasionally seen on APS reports.

The transaminases are quite sensitive to most types of liver damage, from acute inflammation to chronic disease. When both tests are elevated, especially more than minimally, the likelihood of liver impairment is so great that clinical guidelines call for serial testing (repeated tests, at intervals, over time). If the ALT and/or AST do not normalize *and remain normal,* further testing, which could include a liver biopsy, may be done to ascertain the nature and extent of any liver impairment.

In insurance screening, it is not uncommon to encounter individuals with no history of liver disease who have elevations of AST and/or ALT. In those situations, the underwriter will consider a variety of factors in his analysis of the risk.

- Does the individual have any history of hepatitis? Does he have an increased risk for hepatitis? Hepatitis B and C are particularly significant in this regard.

- Has the individual ever been turned away as a blood donor? Why? Has he subsequently been allowed to give blood?

- Is there any evidence of heavy drinking? If there is an isolated AST elevation, it might be prudent for the underwriter to consider ordering a HAA test [discussed under "Alcohol Markers" later in this chapter] to further evaluate the risk.

- Is the proposed insured more than minimally overweight? Many obese individuals will have a fatty liver (hepatic steatosis). In most cases, this condition will be silent, producing no symptoms. Occasionally, however, fatty liver progresses to a form of chronic hepatitis known as NASH (nonalcoholic steatohepatitis). NASH can lead to chronic liver inflammation and even cirrhosis.

- Have there been elevations of AST or ALT in the past? When? How many times? Was that investigated to any extent by the attending physician? What were his findings and recommendations?

- One of the most common genetically-mediated diseases seen (mainly, but not exclusively) in caucasians of Northern European or Celtic ancestry is hereditary hemochromatosis. This disease affects the liver (silently in its early stages), pancreas, heart and other internal organs. ALT elevation often occurs. A family history (mainly in fathers and male siblings) of *both* diabetes *and* cirrhosis/liver cancer raises the spectre of this illness. Fortunately, there are tests readily accessible to the insured's physician that can evaluate patients for possible hereditary hemochromatosis.

- In the case of an isolated AST elevation, is there any reason to suspect a recent muscle injury as the culprit? Trauma from strenuous exercise or an accident can mildly elevate this test for a period of time.

- Is the proposed insured taking any medication that could elevate ALT (more common), AST (less common) or both? The list of such medications is long and includes many commonly prescribed therapeutic drugs (lovastatin for high cholesterol, methotrexate for psoriasis and rheumatoid arthritis, for example). This also might happen with certain medicinal herbs.

One more time: if you do not ask about medications of all kinds during the fact finding interview and when the application is taken, you are asking for problems in scenarios like this!

When AST and ALT are both elevated, the underwriter will look at the one that is more elevated. In many studies, when AST is higher than ALT, the incidence of alcohol abuse has been shown to be heightened. In individuals with transaminase elevations who have chronic hepatitis C or nonalcoholic steatohepatitis—when AST is greater than ALT—the risk of liver cirrhosis is significantly increased.

Gamma-glutamyltransferase (GGT) is the most sensitive test for liver impairment. It is also prone to elevate in individuals who abuse alcohol. Many such persons, especially at younger ages, will not have any evidence of heavy drinking other than an isolated, raised GGT level. GGT can also be elevated by several medications.

GGT may be identified as GGTP and also referred to as gamma-glutamyl transpeptidase. It can become elevated as a result of liver injury, liver disease, impeded bile flow within the liver's duct system or by a mechanism known as enzyme induction. With enzyme induction, a medication or other chemical triggers the release of GGT. Alcohol is strongly associated with this process which explains why GGT is more sensitive to heavy drinking than any other liver function test.

When GGT is elevated in the presence of other abnormal liver tests, the likelihood of a liver or bile duct ailment is greatly increased. This, then, becomes the focus of the underwriter's concern.

Conversely, when GGT elevation is an *isolated* finding, actual liver disease is much less likely to be present. An isolated GGT elevation does not, however, necessarily corrrelate with a favorable underwriting outome because it might be indicative of alcohol abuse.

An individual who reguarly consumes six or more alcoholic drinks per day (a level universally recognized as abuse) has at least a 50 percent probability of an elevated GGT. However, a single binge of drinking will never raise the GGT beyond the normal limit. This has been proven in experiments where volunteers become intoxicated for the sake of scientific research!

If the blood profile shows a GGT elevation and all other liver function tests are normal, the underwriter will look carefully for evidence of alcohol abuse.

- **Is there any history consistent with alcohol abuse?**

- **Are there signs and/or symptoms consistent with possible heavy drinking (or its consequences) on the APS, etc.**

- **Are there alcohol related violations on the driving record?**

The underwriter may order an alcohol marker reflex test to further assess the likelihood of heavy drinking. These tests, known as CDT and HAA respectively, are discussed in detail under the heading "Alcohol Markers."

The other important mechanism accounting for an isolated elevation of GGT is the use of certain therapeutic drugs. There are only a few medications convincingly shown to cause this to happen.

- **Most (but not all) antiseizure/epilepsy drugs, especially hydantoin (Dilantin) and carbamezapine (Tegretol).**

- **Barbiturates, of which only phenobarbital use is seen more than rarely by underwriters.**

- **Warfarin (Coumadin), a blood-thinning medication given mainly in the presence of significant impairments.**

This, once again, underscores the huge importance of making sure all medications currently or recently taken by your client, for any reason, are identified by name on the application or in a cover letter. Be sure to ask your client about non-prescription (over-the-counter) medications and herbal preparations. A few herbs can induce clinicially significant, even life threatening, liver damage. Others may elevate liver enzymes without any symptoms or other objective evidence of liver injury.

Alcohol Markers

In the early 1990s, insurance laboratories began to offer tests known as alcohol markers. Two of these markers are now widely used by insurers as reflex tests to evaluate applicants who present one or more factors that suggest possible alcohol abuse.

One of those markers is hemoglobin-associated acetaldehyde and is referred to as HAA. The other marker is carbohydrate-deficient transferrin and it, too, is referred to as an acronym derived from its full name (CDT).

Transferrin is an iron transport protein. A small percentage of one's transferrin is "carbohydrate-deficient." This portion may be readily quantified and there are several methods available to accomplish this. The only one approved for use by the Food and Drug Administration at this writing calculates both total CDT and also expresses the CDT as a percentage of total transferrin. Other methods are thought to be more vulnerable to false positives, especially in females.

HAA measures the amount of an alcohol metabolite, known as acetaldehyde, bound to the protein hemoglobin. Since the main source of acetaldehyde is alcohol intake, the higher one's HAA, the more likely one is to be a heavy drinker.

Sometimes individuals who have had numerous alcoholic drinks in close proximity to a blood specimen collection will show an increased level of their "free acetaldehyde." This is different from the HAA and is *always* corrected for in the HAA test process. Thus, someone who inadvertantly has had a blood sample collected for insurance testing "the morning after" (a party, for example), should never be mistakenly identified as a possible alcohol abuser based on an HAA test result.

Both HAA and CDT are more sensitive to heavy drinking than liver enzyme tests. If a person consumes six or more drinks per day (which meets most experts' criterion for "abuse"), that individual will likely have an elevated HAA level and/or an elevated CDT level. In some cases, both will be elevated (abnormal); in other cases, both will be within the normal range. Why? *Because, as yet, there is no one lab test that identifies all individuals who abuse alcohol.*

For reasons unrelated to their use in insurance underwriting, the HAA and CDT tests are seldom encountered in clinical medicine. In fact, many physicians will be totally unfamiliar with them. Nonetheless, the database documenting their value as reflex tests for heavy drinking is extensive.

A classic example of an underwriting situation where an alcohol marker can be helpful is an individual who has an isolated elevation of the GGT test. A significant minority of such individuals will be alcohol abusers. Many others will be temperate drinkers or even teetotalers whose GGT is raised because they are taking a prescribed drug or herbal remedy, or via some other mechanism. Simply stated, when an underwriter has a case with an isolated and unexplained GGT elevation, favorable action may be possible *if* an alcohol marker test is normal.

Which leads to another very important point: the ideal test to further assess risk in this setting (isolated, elevated GGT) is, clearly, HAA.

Six major studies, published in leading medical journals devoted to alcoholism research, have all shown that CDT is a reflex test for elevated GGT. This is because GGT and CDT tend to elevate in different subsets of alcohol abusers. An extensive study of individuals who were tested, and whose results were published in the underwriting journal ON THE RISK, revealed that HAA is superior to CDT as a reflex test in the presence of a raised GGT on a screening blood profile.

Two additional underwriting scenarios must be mentioned in the context of alcohol markers.

An applicant who has been convicted of drunk driving (DWI/DUI) has a high probability of being an alcohol abuser. In published studies, the percentage of DWI and DUI convicts who meet established criteria for alcohol abuse/dependency has ranged from 50 percent to as high as 90 percent.

The dominant underwriting response to a drunk driving conviction is to assess a temporary flat extra premium for one or more years. The very strong probability that such an individual is, in fact, still an abusive drinker has considerable mortality risk significance. That can be clarified with alcohol markers. In this context, underwriters may choose to order both CDT and HAA. By doing so, they maximize the likelihood of identifying those applicants with a history of DWI/DUI who continue to drink excessively.

The other situation where alcohol markers are commonly used is applicants with very high HDL-C levels. A man with an HDL-C over 80 mg/dL is at signficant risk for being a heavy drinker. The CDT has been shown to be particularly sensitive to abusive drinking in male subjects with very high HDL-C and, thus, it is CDT that is likely to be used in this context by underwriters.

Prostate Specific Antigen

It is now common, in clinical medicine, for physicians to order a prostate specific antigen (PSA) test on male patients aged 50 and older at the time of their annual physical exam. The PSA is the first "tumor marker" to be used routinely in this manner because an elevation of PSA might be the only clue to an early, curable prostate gland malignancy.

Many insurance companies now screen older male applicants with PSA. If the PSA is normal or only minimally elevated, favorable action is usually taken.

Higher elevations, on the other hand, often mean that the case must be postponed.

Recently, a new reflex test known as % Free PSA has become available. It allows underwriters to approve some cases with an elevated PSA that might otherwise have been postponed.

Many PSA elevations are due to benign causes. One common condition associated with aging and known as benign prostatic hyperplasia (BPH) can cause PSA to mildly elevate. Acute and chronic inflammation of the prostate gland (prostatitis), as well as a precancerous condition called prostatic intraepithelial neoplasia (PIN), may also raise PSA.

At least one study has shown that vigorous exercise can raise PSA perhaps as much as three-fold if that exercise is done shortly before the blood specimen is collected. This is yet another reason for making sure blood is *never* collected within eight hours of any type of sustained or intensive exercise.

If your client is postponed for an elevated PSA test, careful investigation to determine the cause of the elevation (and, above all, to exclude cancer as *the* cause) will likely be undertaken by his physician. Such an evelution may be be done by the attending physician himself or through a referral to a urologist. Whenever this happens (and the results do not obviously preclude issuing insurance!), do your best to have the full details released to the underwriter so the risk can be reevaluated in light of the (presumably) favorable findings.

PSA exists in two main forms: free and bound. The latter refers to PSA that circulates in the bloodstream attached to a protein. When individuals have an elevated PSA, the percentage of their total PSA which is free (i.e., *not* bound to a protein) is a significant indicator of the probability of a prostate malignancy being present.

The test which measures the free portion of PSA is known as the % Free PSA test. Experts have shown this test has great value in pinpointing those men with an elevated total PSA who are most likely to harbor prostate cancer. The % Free PSA might also give physicians some idea of the likelihood of aggressive behavior by prostate cancers in patients who do, in fact, have this malignancy.

The % Free PSA test is now available to underwriters. It is used mainly when a screening PSA falls into what is called the "gray zone" of PSA elevations.

PSA is measured in tiny units called nanograms. In most PSA test protocols, a reading less than 4 nanograms (ng/mL) is normal. Conversely, if PSA is at least 10 nanograms, studies have shown a significant probability of prostate cancer. Thus, it is an individiual whose screening PSA falls between 4 and 10 (the "gray zone") who is apt to be deemed a possible candidate for reflex testing using the % Free PSA test.

Urine Tests

Decades before life underwriters worried over the meaning of elevated GGTs, urine specimens were being dutifully collected by agents and sent to home offices for analysis. In those days, the focus of the urinalysis was apt to be on traditional, clinical components such as protein and blood cells. Today, the four major "pay-offs" from urine testing are tests for evidence of two psychoactive drugs (nicotine and cocaine), for small amounts of urinary albumin (the microalbumin test) and the urine HIV test.

Unlike blood samples that must be taken by trained technicians, urine specimens can readily be collected by agents. The longtime practice of agent collected urine gave way to collection by paramedical technicians in the 1970s. More recently, however, there has been a substantial return to agent collected urine, especially where urine testing has been used in lieu of blood testing at younger ages and on smaller amounts of coverage.

The contemporary urine profile in life underwriting consists of three components:

1. routine urinalysis;

2. adulterant screening; and

3. so-called "special testing."

Routine Urinalysis

This component of the insurance sensitive urine profile includes tests for protein, glucose (sugar), red blood cells, white blood cells and casts. These are also the main ingredients in a *clinical* urinalysis.

Protein in the Urine

The presence of protein in the urine might be the first sign of a potentially life-threatening kidney impairment such as chronic glomerulonephritis or diabetic nephropathy. At the other extreme, protein might pass through the kidney's filter as a result of exercise or low-grade fever.

The screening test for proteinuria is often done using a method referred to as a "dipstick" test. This technique, which relies on a color change reaction, is fast and sensitive to small quantities of protein. However, the dipstick technique cannot distinguish between the most important type of protein (albumin) and other less important urinary proteins. For this reason, underwriters will often order a microalbumin (MA) reflex test whenever proteinuria is discovered on a screening test. The MA test, which may be performed on the original urine specimen, quantifies only the albumin portion of urine protein.

As indicated above, proteinuria can occur in healthy individuals due to transient causes. Thus, when proteinuria is discovered in a screening specimen, underwriters may choose to order one or even two additional urine specimens, typically with the added instruction that they be collected on rising in the morning and on separate days. The caveat "on rising" assures that exercise will not be a cause of further proteinuria (except in athletic somnambulists!). Collecting additional specimens on separate days maximizes the likelihood that, if the applicant is free of kidney impairment, the additional specimens will be normal. Therefore, it is to your client's advantage that you promtly arrange for collection of the needed additional specimens.

If the amount of proteinuria is more than minimal, if it is found in several specimens and/or if the microalbumin (MA) test is also positive, adverse underwriting action is likely. This is especially true if the applicant has a history of an impairment, such as diabetes or high blood pressure, associated with insidious kidney damage.

It is now routine for underwriters to order a microalbumin (MA) test on all applicants with diabetes, a prediabetic condition such as impaired glucose tolerance or impaired fasting glucose, an unexplained high blood sugar level on a current blood profile or a history of longstanding hypertension. In addition, the MA test is being seen by cardiologists as a marker for coronary artery disease, especially in middle-aged and older persons. For those reasons, the use of the MA test has greatly increased in life underwriting.

Whenever unexpected proteinuria leads to adverse action, it is to the client's advantage to have the insurance test findings passed along to his personal physician. There are two reasons for this.

1. **If symptomless kidney damage is present, early discovery could lead to successful treatment.**

2. **If further testing fails to disclose evidence of a significant condition, eligibility for insurance is almost always enhanced.**

As noted above, physical exercise can induce both proteinuria and microalbuminuria. It is important to caution the client against any significant exercise for *at least* several hours prior to urine specimen collection. It is also important not to collect the urine specimen if the proposed insured has a fever, as might be the case with a cold or upper respiratory infection.

Glucose (Sugar) in the Urine

The presence of sugar in the urine, called glycosuria, can be associated with chronically high blood sugar levels. That, in turn, is apt to be due to diabetes mellitus.

There are other conditions that can cause glycosuria, such as pregnancy, a harmless disturbance dubbed "renal glycosuria" (which has no effect on insurability whatsoever) and, in some individuals, simply a high intake of sweets prior to specimen collection. This last scenario is very avoidable. Whenever possible, urine specimens should not be collected within two hours of eating a meal or foraging on sweet snacks.

Blood Cells in the Urine

Routine urinalysis looks for evidence of both red and white blood cells in the urine. The significance of those two findings, however, could not be more different.

Hematuria (red blood cells in the urine) can be the first sign of an undiscovered kidney or bladder cancer. However, the vast majority of episodes of hematuria are due to transient/benign causes. The underwriting of hematuria is influenced by several key factors.

- **Age of the applicant. Cancer is overwhelmingly a disease of aging. Hematuria that is not investigated will be underwritten more cautiously at older ages.**

- **Hematuria in more than one specimen. Underwriters are inclined to order additional urine specimens when hematuria is discovered unexpectedly.**

- **Any history of kidney or urinary tract impairments. A tendency to form kidney stones, chronic kidney inflammation (glomerulonephritis), etc., adds to the significance of current hematuria.**

- **Significant proteinuria or microalbuminuria in addition to hematuria.**

- **Risk factors for kidney and urinary tract cancers including longtime cigarette smoking.**

Evidence of white blood cells in the urine (pyuria) is not nearly so signficant as hematuria because most pyuria is only temporary and due to lower urinary tract or prostate gland infection. Unless the volume of white blood cells is unusually high or there are other adverse findings, underwriting should be favorable.

Casts in the Urine

A cast is a tiny bit of hardened protein that is formed in the kidney's tubules. The finding of casts in the urine is called cylindruria.

The most common type of cast is the hyaline cast. In normal individuals, hyaline casts will be detected after physical exercise. The same is true for the next most prevalent type of cast—the granular cast. A granular cast simply is a hyaline cast with cellular debris embedded in it. Most individuals showing only hyaline and/or granular casts as isolated findings on a routine urinalysis will be free of renal impairment.

Other types of casts might be much more significant. They are also distinctly uncommon in otherwise healthy persons.

Adulterant Screening and Chain of Custody

It is necessary for laboratories to have a special battery of tests designed to detect specimen tampering. These tests pinpoint any interfering substances added to the urine specimens to hamper or distort analysis. Specimen dilution, caused by drinking large quantities of fluids shortly before voiding a specimen, is also easily unmasked.

Another concern addressed by adulterant screening is specimen substitution. This is done by checking the temperature immediately upon specimen collection. At voiding, urine is certain to be at a temperature within a fairly narrow range.

Any deviation means the urine was substituted (or the specimen donor is a reanimated corpse!).

All laboratories have in place elaborate "chain of custody" procedures to assure that the specimen voided by a particular individual is, indeed, the one attributed to that person on the test report. In insurance testing, these procedures include the use of multiple signatures, detailed handling practices, careful container labeling (which might include bar coding), etc. The net result of the state of the art chain of custody procedures is that mixups in handling are extraordinarily rare events.

Special Urine Testing

This component of insurance urine testing consists of four categories:

1. **HIV;**
2. **therapeutic drugs;**
3. **drugs of abuse (chiefly cocaine); and**
4. **cotinine (nicotine).**

Both screening (ELISA) and confirmatory (western blot) urine HIV testing is now approved by the Food and Drug Administration. As expected, a growing share of insurance HIV testing is being performed on urine specimens.

Several categories of widely-prescribed therapeutic drugs are sometimes tested for in urine specimens. The main reason for that is to identify individuals taking medications who do not acknowledge their use on the application. Medications sometimes tested for include several classes of antihypertensive drugs (diuretics, beta blockers) as well as oral agents used to treat type 2 diabetics.

Although insurance testing laboratories have the technology to perform sophisticated tests for many drugs of abuse, including heroin, marijuana, phencyclidine (PCP, "angel dust") and methamphetamine ("speed"), the fact is that only one major drug of abuse is routinely tested for in the North American market. That drug is cocaine.

Cocaine Testing

Starting in the 1980s, North America has experienced what experts call an epidemic of cocaine abuse. This potent, highly addictive stimulant can be consumed in a variety of ways, the most popular of which are snorting (intranasal), injection and smoking. In its smokable form, cocaine is often referred to by the street name "crack."

There is a widely-held misperception that, for the most part, the kind of people who abuse cocaine do not buy much life insurance. This is quickly corrected by reviewing demographic reports of subjects who have had positive cocaine tests (or, simply, by reading the newspapers!).

Cocaine testing begins with a screening test that is designed to be highly sensitive. This means it is capable of detecting the vast majority of individuals who have recently ingested cocaine in any form.

Urine specimens testing positive on this screening test are then confirmed as "true positives" using a second, very different procedure. The confirmatory test of choice is known as gas chromatography with mass spectrometry (GC/MS). It is recognized as the "gold standard" for drug testing. When the GC/MS test is used to confirm a positive cocaine screening test, the possibility of a false test is virtually eliminated.

Cocaine itself is rapidly metabolized by the body, having a "half life" in the bloodstream of only 30 minutes. However, one major metabolite of cocaine, benzoylecgonine (BNZ), is detectable for a minimum of 3 to 5 days after cocaine was last used. In reports from treatment programs, it has been shown that tests for cocaine use can be positive for several weeks or even longer in heavy users and recovering addicts.

When an insurance applicant tests positive for cocaine use, coverage will seldom be approved on any basis. This may lead to a challenge as to the validity of the test result, with the proposed insured insisting that he did not, in fact, use cocaine.

If the trail of the specimen, from collection to testing at the laboratory, is consistent with an intact chain of custody, and certainly whereever confirmation was done with the GC/MS test procedure, there is virtually no margin for error.

However, there might be a legitimate reason for the positive cocaine tests, one that does not compromise insurability in any way. Indeed, the proposed insured may not even be aware of the circumstances that put him at risk for a positive test!

Cocaine is used as an anesthetic in certain surgical procedures. These can include surgeries to the mouth, nose, nasal sinuses and eyes, and the treatment of facial lacerations and abrasions in the emergency room. The patient receiving a cocaine-based anesthetic might not be told, or might not recall, that cocaine was part of the anesthetizing compound he was administered. Cocaine may be just one component in a multicomponent anesthetic compound such as TAC (short for tatracaine, adrenaline and cocaine).

Therefore, if your client is declined because of a positive cocaine test, there is *one question* worth raising with him: "Did you, within the immediate several days prior to the time you gave the urine or oral fluid specimen for insurance, receive an anesthetic administered by a physician or oral surgeon?" If the answer is YES, provide your underwriter with a statement from the client that includes the type of surgery, the date of the procedure and the name and address of the physician who performed it. Understand that the underwriter must confirm the facts with this physician.

Another theoretical "defense" for a positive cocaine test is the use of cocaine-laced herbal teas. Importation of such teas is illegal although there are supposed to be decocainized versions of these teas available in North America. "Decocainized" means that the cocoa (cocaine) has been removed. However, as in decaffeinated coffees, small residual amounts of the purged substance may linger. This is, at best, an extremely improbable and dubious explanation for a positive cocaine screening test. When doubt exists, consider asking the insurance lab to test a tea bag alleged to contain "decocainized" coca tea. The answer to the question "Could consuming this tea have caused the positive cocaine test?" should be readily apparent from such additional, specific testing.

Cocaine Hair Testing

The technology exists to test hair specimens for the presence of a variety of substances, including heavy metals such as lead and various drugs of abuse. Such testing is possible because some substances, once ingested, become permanently embedded in the hair. They cannot be washed out and do not diminish with time.

The only substance for which hair specimens are tested in underwriting is cocaine. An underwriter will resort to this test only on very rare occasions as the hair test is not more reliable or more valid than the urine or oral fluid cocaine test. However, the hair test does confer one distinct advantage, what pathologists call a "long window of detection." Even if the last cocaine use was weeks prior to the time of hair sample collection, telltale evidence (immune to hair washing, hair dyeing, etc.) can still be found.

Cotinine (Nicotine) Testing

In the early 1980s, spurred on by a number of insurance mortality studies that showed distinctly higher death rates among cigarette smokers, insurers began to ask cigarette smokers to pay higher premiums than cigarette abstainers. More recently, the "cigarette only" approach has begun to give way to what is now commonly called "user/abstainer" pricing (tobacco use in all of its forms vs. tobacco abstention).

All proposed insureds are carefully questioned about tobacco use on the application. Unfortunately, some individuals willfully misrepresent their tobacco use proclivities in hopes of qualifying for lower premium rates. A decade of industry experience has shown that as many as 3 percent to 7 percent of applicants could suffer from what is labeled as "smoker's amnesia"! The antidote for this is the cotinine test.

Although often referred to as a "nicotine test," this test actually measures nicotine's main metabolite, cotinine. Nicotine is a tenaciously addicting psychoactive drug with a very short life span in the body; it is rapidly converted into cotinine. Cotinine remains in the body much longer, making it an ideal substance to screen for tobacco use.

This raises one of the most common questions asked of underwriters by producers: How long, measured from the last tobacco use, will the cotinine test remain positive?

A number of factors influence the metabolizing of nicotine into cotinine and its subsequent clearance from the body. Among the factors are the amount of tobacco consumed, the form in which it is used, the presence of other substances which might compete for the use of metabolizing enzymes, that cotinine is fat soluble and can persist longer in persons who are obese, as well as the state of hydration of the individual. These and other factors explain why one individual will have a negative cotinine test just one or two days after his last cigarette, while another smoker will remain positive for three or four days; it is rarely longer than that.

Anything that contains tobacco contains nicotine. Thus, pipe smokers, cigar smokers and oral tobacco users will all have cotinine in their urine. The same is true for individuals who use nicotine-laced chewing gum or use a transdermal nicotine patch, almost always in an effort to kick their tobacco habit. The only other significant source of nicotine (and, thus, cotinine) presents a highly improbable scenario: heavy and very direct exposure to certain agricultural herbicides derived from tobacco.

A recent study undertaken by a major insurance testing lab showed that there is one significant exception to the rule which states that users will test positive for cotinine. Individuals who smoked *but did not inhale* one large cigar were found to test negative for cotinine on both urine and oral fluid tests at 30 minutes, 12 hours and 24 hours after smoking that one cigar.

The implications are important because many insurers now allow a (strictly defined) "occasional" cigar smoker, especially one who has never smoked cigarettes, to qualify as a "nonuser" of tobacco for underwriting purposes. This practice makes sense to us because there is no evidence that smoking a (very) occasional cigar, without inhaling, is associated with significant excess mortality or morbidity.

In recent years, research has convincingly shown that chronic exposure to tobacco smoke by nonsmokers, especially in poorly ventilated environments, is harmful. Indeed, so-called "passive smoking" has been linked to health consequences ranging from frequent respiratory symptoms in asthmatic children to lung cancers in the nonsmoking spouses of heavy cigarette smokers.

Will "passive smokers" have measurable quantities of cotinine in their urine? Absolutely. However, this answer is deceiving in an underwriting context. The threshold level of cotinine required for a positive insurance test has been intentionally set several times higher than the highest level of cotinine ever recorded in any "passive smoker!" The bottom line is that "passive smoking" is never a valid explanation for a positive test in an ostensibly "nonsmoking" applicant.

The practice of cosuming so-called betel (or areca) nut is common in India and also in most other Asian countries. Persons who emigrate from Asia often continue their consumption of betel nut in North America.

Betel nut is seeds of the Areca catechu plant and is sometimes consumed with tobacco. Even if that is not the case, research has shown that certain substances in betel nut, known as alkaloids, can sometimes cause a positive cotinine test.

A growing number of insurers consider the use of betel nut to be the equivalent to tobacco use for underwriting purposes because, like oral tobacco products, betel nut is strongly associated with mouth cancer. In addition, betel nut has been shown to induce stomach cancer in some chronic users. An addicting drug, betel nut has also been linked to cardiovascular impairment.

Bidis (pronounced "beedies") are a type of unfiltered cigarette from India that is said to be widely sold in convenience stores (and even some health food stores!) in North America. They come in many flavors but the fact is their main ingredient is tobacco. They resemble marijuana joints and have become a popular fad in some places. What's the bottom line? Bidis are cigarettes and users must be treated as smokers for underwriting purposes.

Some vegetables are known to contain minute quantities of nicotine. However, consumption of *normal* quantities of these vegetables will not result in a positive cotinine test. For example, eggplant is higher in nicotine content (concentrated in the peel) than most vegetables. Research has shown that to consume the quantity of nicotine needed to produce a positive cotinine test at the test thresholds used by life insurers, one would have to eat three to five kilograms of raw, unpeeled eggplant. So much for the "ratatouille defense"!

Although the majority of insurance cotinine testing is performed on urine specimens, cotinine is also readily detectable in blood and oral fluid samples. Serum (blood) cotinine tests are sometimes ordered as reflex tests to confirm the presence of cotinine in a scenario where the applicant loudly protests, arguing that his urine specimen must have been "mixed up at the lab." Oral fluid cotinine testing is widespread and growing in the insurance industry.

Oral Fluid ("Saliva") Testing

The technology exists to perform certain insurance tests using an oral fluid specimen. A more appropriate term for the oral fluid collected in this "saliva" test is mucosal transudate. Mucosal transudate is not saliva. To avoid confusion, we will simply use the term "oral fluid" to denote mucosal transudate collected for insurance testing.

The very idea of testing oral fluid conjures up the unpleasant image of someone being asked to spit into a bottle! In fact, the method of collection is actually much more client friendly than having blood drawn. The technique involves gently stimulating the gum line with a soft pad on a toothbrush-like device. The tip is then inserted into a specimen container, the handle snapped off, the container sealed and then mailed or couriered to the lab.

HIV testing on oral fluid is every bit as reliable as on blood or urine. It is also possible to test oral fluid for cotinine (nicotine) and cocaine, with results comparable to those obtained with urine specimens. Oral fluid testing for hepatitis B surface antigen and for antibodies to the hepatitis C virus was introduced in the late 1990s. There is hope that further oral fluid test components will become available to insurers in the years ahead.

Oral fluid testing now plays a major role in underwriting, domestically and internationally. With the increasing focus on turnaround time (that is, the interval from application to policy issue), many insurers have opted to raise their blood test thresholds, mainly at ages 45 and under, and to use either oral fluid or urine instead of blood testing, mainly on smaller amounts of insurance. Indeed, the low cost, ease of collection and high accuracy of oral fluid tests creates the potential, at least, for universal screening of all individually underwritten life insurance applications.

In many cases, oral fluid (and, increasingly, urine) specimens are collected by the producer at the time the application is completed. Agent collection maximizes turnaround time and greatly helps control acquisition expenses for insurers. Thus, producers are well served when they collect oral fluid and urine samples for underwriting purposes.

Wellness Programs

In the 1980s, lab tests became a predominant part of the medical underwriting screening undertaken by life and disability insurers. In the 1990s, the same blood, urine and oral fluid test information gathered from the client was repackaged and sent back to the client. These feedback loops are now known as "wellness programs."

This client friendly innovation assures that the insurance buyer gets the benefit of the lab test results every bit as much as the underwriter. It is less of an annoyance to have your blood drawn if you see the results. In some cases, the client will be alerted to, for example, a higher than ideal cholesterol level. Consequently, he will take measures to lower that number. Also, he will remember how he learned about the problem–the wellness report his agent or broker had the insurance company send him.

The typical wellness program consists of a report of the blood profile results, comfortably formatted for a lay reader, together with easy-to-understand information amplifying the meaning of the tests, etc. In some programs, the client's attention to good health is reinforced with a short term, free subscription to a "good health" magazine. The wellness package is either delivered by the agent or mailed from the home office after the policy is placed in force.

Other Medical Tests

Electrocardiogram

Whether you prefer to call them EKGs or ECGs, you must be familiar with electrocardiograms. ECG age and amount limits have been liberalized dramatically in recent years, especially at younger ages. Still, the ECG remains the second most widely used medical underwriting screening test after the lab profile.

ECG screening thresholds tend to drop steeply with advancing age. This is shown in a 1994 underwriting survey of 234 North American life insurers. At age 25, 60 percent of the companies indicated they did not require a resting ECG until the face amount of the policy was over $500,000. Compare that to age 65 where the most prevalent ECG screening threshold was $100,000 and 30 percent of the companies actually began screening below that amount.

Why are ECG screening limits so steeply graded by age? Because the ECG is, first and foremost, a screening test for coronary artery disease and the prevalence of coronary disease rises steeply with age.

The resting 12-lead electrocardiogram, which is the standard form of the test used by insurers, might be defined as a graphic representation of the electrical activity of the heart. The heart has its own electrical system that generates the heart beat and which incites the muscular contractions of the heart muscle which, in turn, pumps the blood!

The ECG portrays this electrical activity as two-dimensional deflections from a baseline. There are five main deflections known as the P, Q, R, S and T waves.

When one interprets an ECG, the height or depth of these waves is measured. The ECG can also be seen as a series of segments, starting or stopping with certain deflections. The duration of these segments and the extent of these deflections are keys to deciding if the ECG is normal or abnormal.

A significant number of screening ECGs are, technically, abnormal. That does not mean, however, that they are doomed to be rated. In fact, the vast majority of "abnormal" ECGs have trivial abnormalities of no importance in underwriting.

Every underwriting manual mentions over a hundred distinct electrocardiographic abnormalities. These range from those typically taken "standard," such as the first degree heart block and paroxysmal atrial tachycardia, to those where adverse action is all but assured, such as Mobitz II heart block, left bundle branch block or ventricular tachycardia. Some of the more commonly encountered, potentially significant abnormal ECG findings include:

- **Second and third degree heart blocks. In second degree heart blocks, some electrical impulses from the upper chambers of the heart (atria) do not conduct through the electrical system to the lower chambers (ventricles).**

  There are two forms of second degree heart block: Mobitz I and Mobitz II. The latter is seldom seen in nondiseased hearts.

  In a third degree, or complete, heart block, there are no electrical impulses conducted between the atria and the ventricles; they beat separately. Problems that develop might eventually lead to installing a cardiac pacemaker.

- **Left bundle branch block (LBBB). In this form of heart block, electrical impulses cannot reach the all-important left ventricle by their normal route. Unlike right bundle branch blocks, which are seldom rated, the LBBB must be seen as evidence of heart impairment and subject to further testing.**

- **Left ventricular hypertrophy (LVH). Enlargement of the left ventricle, due to longstanding hypertension or a heart disorder, has been shown to be a significant indicator of excess mortality. Unfortunately, the ECG is limited in its ability to pinpoint early LVH with great accuracy. An echocardiogram is ideal for that purpose.**

- **Premature ventricular contractions (PVCs). PVCs are common and everyone gets them, from caffeine, stress, etc. They are described as simple or complex. Simple PVCs are usually overlooked unless they are very numerous. Complex PVCs, on the other hand, might be a clue to underlying cardiac impairment. Clinical physicians may further test patients who have complex PVCs. In most cases, they will order what is called a Holter monitor. This is a continuous ECG tracing that is recorded nonstop for many hours.**

- **Atrial fibrillation. This is a very rapid and highly irregular electrical pattern arising in the upper heart chambers (atria). There are two main types of atrial fibrillation: paroxysmal (sudden) and chronic. The paroxysmal form, often simply called PAF, can arise unexpectedly at any age. Most individuals with PAF do not have underlying heart disease. A bout of heavy drinking is a common cause in young adults. In its chronic form, atrial fibrillation is almost always due to a significant heart condition.**

- **Major T wave changes. T waves are the last upward deflection on most ECG tracings. If flattened or slightly inverted, T waves are said to have minor changes. These changes are seldom acted upon adversely as an isolated finding. However, if T waves are upside down (major changes), studies have shown significant excess mortality.**

- **Q waves. Q waves are downward deflections on the ECG and they should be present in some places on the ECG tracing. In others, they might signify what is called an "electrically dead" area of the heart, due to a previous myocardial infarction, etc. Suffice it to say that underwriting abnormal Q waves is a challenge even for experienced underwriters and medical directors.**

If a resting ECG has abnormalities suggestive of decreased oxygen flow to the heart muscle (myocardial ischemia), the underwriter may order a treadmill stress test to further evaluate the applicant. A normal treadmill test in this context usually results in a favorable underwriting decision.

Further assessment of the significance of some adverse ECG findings, like the left bundle branch block, might require expensive, additional testing (myocardial perfusion scan, using a radioisotope such as thallium or technetium, echocardiogram, etc.). If your client's personal physician undertakes such testing *and* if the results are said to be favorable, make sure those results get to the underwriter. In many cases, the risk can be seen in a more favorable light.

Sometimes, the first question that comes to mind when we see an abnormality on a resting ECG is: Is this a change or has it always been present? Changes imply (but do not confirm) a heart problem. A stable abnormality, present for years, might be treated more liberally. Thus, the underwriter may seek to borrow historic ECG tracings. If he succeeds, the outlook brightens from the producer's perspective. However, if you do not know whether an ECG abnormality is a recent change or has been present throughout the client's entire life, you must take a conservative approach.

Performing an ECG is easy; interpreting it may not be that easy. While garden variety abnormalities can be spotted and correctly labeled by a screener, there are others that are more subtle or complicated, so much so that sometimes cardiologists will disagree as to what is present. The same is true with regard to a subjective assessment of the significance of some abnormalities. From an underwriting perspective, major T wave changes are usually incompatible with a favorable decision. From the clinical perspective, they may be characterized to the patient in an entirely different light. It all comes down to the differences between clinical and insurance medicine.

Chest X-ray

There was a time when the chest x-ray was a common requirement—that time has passed. For many good reasons, the use of the screening chest x-ray has declined dramatically in underwriting. The view from here is that this should continue until no screening chest x-rays are required routinely for underwriting.

When we think of chest x-rays, we think of identifying lung disease or an unsuspected cancer. In fact, most medical directors agree that it is heart size, not lung disease, that gives chest x-rays much of their value. The ECG changes in heart enlargement are notoriously insensitive and nonspecific. The test of choice, the echocardiogram, is too expensive for regular use in risk appraisal. In this setting, therefore, the elective use of a chest x-ray to ascertain heart size might be an appropriate choice.

On those rare occasions when something potentially sinister is spotted on a chest x-ray, there are few options open to the underwriter. Most cases must be postponed pending a clinical workup. If the possibility of chronic obstructive lung disease is entertained, the logical next test is pulmonary function testing (PFTs, spirometry). This test can be done by paramedical companies and many MD examiners.

Treadmill Stress Test

Also commonly referred to by underwriters simply as exercise ECGs, treadmill stress tests are routinely used to screen large amount cases. While this requirement is usually brought to bear at relatively high face amount thresholds at younger ages, limits can be set lower at ages 60 and over.

Most exercise ECGs, clinically and for insurance, are performed using a treadmill or, on occasion, a stationary bicycle (bicycle ergometer). In the treadmill test protocol, the subject walks on the treadmill while both its slope and speed are increased in stages. This, in turn, causes the subject's workload (and, thus, heart rate) to increase. The same result is accomplished using bicycle ergometry.

The reason treadmill tests are accepted as life insurance screening tests is that they have an increased sensitivity to and specificity for coronary artery disease as compared to resting ECGs. However, when an exercise ECG is said to be positive (abnormal), the underwriter considers the context of the case.

A premenopausal, nonsmoking female is extremely unlikely to have significant coronary disease. A 60 year-old diabetic male who smokes three packs a day and has chest pains while shoveling snow is another matter. In the first scenario, a positive stress test might be underwritten (surprisingly) favorably. In the latter setting, a positive treadmill test will be seen as confirming what the medical history makes one suspect—that the proposed insured has coronary artery disease.

Interpreting a treadmill test is a complicated undertaking. Whereas the commonly-accepted, basic criteria for a "positive" test are fairly straightforward, the proper analysis of all test parameters (ECG tracings, heart rate attained, duration of exercise, blood pressure response, symptoms, if any, etc.), requires considerable training and experience.

It is no surprise that even cardiologists often disagree on whether a given test is "normal" or "abnormal," or on what the prognostic/risk implications are of an agreed upon "abnormal" treadmill test. Many times, the ECG tracings are said to be "within normal limits" but other aspects of the test have unfavorable implications. Examples include the failure to attain a sufficient heart rate, having an abnormal blood pressure response (for instance, systolic blood pressure does not rise with exercise or, there is a sudden drop in blood pressure when the exercise peaks) and the onset of certain symptoms (chest pain, dizziness, irregular heartbeat) with the exercise.

Exercise Myocardial Perfusion Imaging

The underwriting value of the treadmill stress test can be enhanced by performing it in conjunction with a heart scan using a radioisotope, such as thallium-201 or technetium-99. If an individual at low risk for coronary disease (based upon his age and risk factor profile) has an abnormal treadmill stress test, a negative radioisotope scan will, in many cases, put the risk in a more favorable light.

In addition, there are situations where a resting ECG abnormality (left bundle branch block, Wolff-Parkinson-White (WPW) syndrome) renders treadmill stress test ECG tracings uninterpretable. In such situations, the addition of the myocardial perfusion scan is often essential to getting a full perspective on the risk.

The advantages of perfusion imaging in the clinical diagnosis and evaluation of coronary disease are considerable. The same cannot be said for its use in life insurance medicine without recognizing a major limiting factor—cost. These scans are far more expensive than other medical underwriting tests.

Echocardiogram

The echocardiogram is another example of a test that has great appeal to the underwriter because of what it can contribute to assessing the risk. Balanced against this, however, is the matter of cost. Echocardiograms are expensive.

The value of the echocardiogram is made clear by describing what the test does. The echocardiogram is a noninvasive procedure. A device called a transducer, which emits sound waves, is passed over the chest wall to create a sound wave "picture" of the heart. It allows for measurement of heart chamber sizes and wall thicknesses, it gives a view of cardiac valve anatomy and function and more.

The echocardiogram is the test of choice in the further assessment of heart murmurs heard via the medical examiner's stethoscope and of presumed heart enlargement detected during the exam, on the ECG or on the chest x-ray. Most medical clinics and hospitals have facilities to perform echocardiograms; only the cost mitigates against their wider use in evaluating heart murmurs and heart enlargement in underwriting.

The exercise echocardiogram has gained great favor with cardiologists in recent years because it represents an alternative to myocardial perfusion imaging in the further evaluation of persons with positive treadmill stress tests. As in the case of a thallium or technetium scan, a normal exercise echocardiogram can empower the underwriter to look much more favorably on many cases that have an abnormal treadmill test.

Pulmonary Function Testing

The best test to identify chronic obstructive pulmonary disease (COPD) (emphysema, chronic bronchitis) is not a chest x-ray but a test of, literally, one's capacity to breathe. The technical name for this is pulmonary function testing.

The technique is called spirometry and sometimes one may be asked to have "spirometry" performed on a client. Underwriters may also refer to pulmonary function tests simply as a "TVC" or as "PFTs."

Pulmonary function testing, in a clinical setting, might be elaborate (and expensive), consisting of dozens of distinct components. Most of these components would not contribute much additional, useful information in an underwriting context so underwriters generally limit their requests for PFTs to three components:

1. **Forced vital capacity (FVC). This is the amount of air the subject can expel on a single, maximum effort.**

2. **Forced expiratory volume at one second (FEV-1). The amount of air that is expelled during the first second of that effort.**

3. **Midflow rate. There are several tests that measure the amount of air expelled during the middle portion of the expiratory effort. This air comes from the small airways in the lungs. Abnormal midflow rates can be a harbinger of future COPD, etc.**

In addition to looking individually at the results of these three tests, the underwriter also pays close attention to the relationship between the FVC and FEV-1. This relationship is typically referred to as the "timed vital capacity" (TVC): FEV-1/FVC = TVC.

The predominant reason for ordering PFTs is suspected chronic obstructive lung disease (COPD). There are two major components to COPD:

1. **chronic inflammation of the airways (chronic bronchitis); and**

2. **destruction of the air sacs in the lungs (emphysema).**

As COPD progresses, FVC might remain normal or even, paradoxically, increase. However, the telltale findings of diminished FEV-1 and reduced TVC are ominous.

It has been said that pulmonary function testing is the best tool underwriters have for measuring biological age. Chronological age is how old you are based upon when you were born. Biological age is how old your body is based upon your health habits, genetic endowment, etc. Clearly, some people are younger biologically than they are chronologically. The reverse is also true. Pulmonary function tests come closer than any other underwriting requirement to measuring biological age.

There are, however, drawbacks to pulmonary function testing that limits their use in screening. One of those drawbacks is that the test is "effort dependent." The subject needs to blow like the big bad wolf trying to dislodge the pigs from the brick house! Anything less could produce misleading results. Pulmonary function testing is also not cheap. To justify the cost, they are used electively by most insurers only in cases where COPD or some other significant lung disease is suspected. To use them as screening tests would be costly and their predominant value would be focused on one small subset of applicants, for example, longtime, heavy cigarette smokers over age 50.

Complete Blood Count

The complete blood count (CBC) is just what the name implies. It is a qualitative and quantitative measurement of red blood cells, white blood cells and platelets. It is probably the most widely used lab test in clinical medicine.

Producers will seldom see a request for a CBC that needs to be completed on their client. There are numerous scenarios where an underwriter might call for a CBC. When one is needed, it can be a result of information in the medical history or current findings on other requirements. The procedure is relatively inexpensive and it can be performed on blood specimens collected by paramedical vendors and sent to insurance laboratories. The only caveat is that delays in transporting such specimens might result in problems with the analysis of certain CBC components.

The underwriter may specify which CBC components he wants included when the test is performed on a pending case. If the components are not stated specifically, the following list should be satisfactory in most underwriting settings.

- **Red blood cell count.**

- **Hemoglobin (Hg).**

- **Hematocrit (HCT).**

- **Mean corpuscular volume (MCV).**

- **White blood cell count.**

- **White blood cell differential.**

- **Platelet count.**

Hepatitis B and C Testing

It has been estimated that as many as 4 million Americans are infected with the hepatitis C virus. Most of them will not clear this virus with their own immune system and will, therefore, go on to develop chronic hepatitis C. It is currently held that at least 1 in 5 perons with chronic hepatitis C will develop clinically evident cirrhosis of the liver.

Add to that the considerable incidence of hepatitis B in insurance buying populations and it is easy to understand why both hepatitis B and hepatitis C testing have increased dramatically in underwriting.

Hepatitis B and C tests are relatively inexpensive. They are readily available from insurance laboratories using blood, oral fluid and, potentially, urine specimens. Most importantly, they are key to risk assessment if the proposed insured is either a carrier of, or has the chronic form of, hepatitis B or hepatitis C.

The typical insurance hepatitis screening panel consists of two tests:

1. **hepatitis B surface antigen (HBsAg); and**

2. **hepatitis C antibody test (anti-HCV).**

If the proposed insured tests positive for the hepatitis B surface antigen, the insurance laboratory will likely perform an additional test known as the hepatitis

B "e" antigen test. This is often positive in hepatitis B infected individuals when the virus is actively replicating and, thus, prone to cause overt liver damage.

Hepatitis B tests are typically ordered by underwriters if the proposed insured has risk factors for infection with this virus, especially if that individual also has an elevated ALT (SGPT) liver enzyme on the screening blood profile. Due to the growing concern for the implications of hepatitis C, many companies now routinely test for hepatitis C antibodies whenever a proposed insured has a raised ALT level.

CHAPTER 6

Common Problems in Medical Underwriting

Coronary Artery Disease

The leading cause of death in Western society, implicated in over 600,000 deaths in the United States each year, has no fewer than three names. The life underwriter is apt to see all three in the course of his work:

1. **Coronary artery disease (CAD);**

2. **Coronary heart disease (CHD);**

3. **Atherosclerotic heart disease (ASHD).**

Considering that the hallmark lesion is called an atheroma and that it arises within the coronary arteries that bring oxygen bearing blood as nourishment to the heart muscle, perhaps the best name for this disease would be "atherosclerotic coronary artery disease." That would mean, however, adding *another* term of reference and *another* abbreviation (ACAD) to the lexicon of medical science. So, we will just call this disease CAD in his book.

Coronary artery disease can manifest itself as a clinical event in one of two ways:

1. **typical (or not-so-typical) chest pains known as angina pectoris; or**

2. **as a sudden blood flow obstruction that results either in the syndrome known as "unstable angina" or in an acute myocardial infarction, or heart attack.**

Angina pectoris is defined as chest pains provoked by a reduction in oxygen flow to the heart muscle (ischemia) due, in most but not all cases, to partially blocked coronary arteries. These chests pains are usually provoked by exertion or the equivalent, and are relieved by rest and/or certain medications, most notably nitroglycerin.

Unstable angina used to be called acute coronary insufficiency. It is brought on by a sudden and significant increase in the extent of coronary artery blockage, usually due to the formation of a thrombus (blood clot) in the artery. It differs from a heart attack mainly in that the artery is not completely closed off to the blood flow and also because there is no residual, permanent damage to the heart muscle.

Myocardial infarction (MI) is the medical term for "heart attack." The blood supply to a portion of the heart muscle is cut off long enough to produce a sequence of events culminating in the death of that part of the muscle. The inciting event is a sudden, complete obstruction of a coronary artery segment, again, usually by vitrue of a blood clot. Most fatalities resulting from acute MIs are caused by cardiac electrical disturbances (ventricular arrythmias) that degenerate into lethal ventricular fibrillation.

The most common medical history event that raises suspicion for CAD is chest pain. When a prospective insured has a history of chest pain, the underwriter will be tenacious in seeking out the details. The producer can assist the underwriter and speed up the selection process (and possibly avoid redundant requirements) by making sure that the chest pain history is fully detailed on the Part II or an accompanying medical history statement.

These are the questions the underwriter must answer concerning any potentially significant history of chest pain(s):

- **What brought on the attack(s)?**

- **What brought relief from the attack(s)?**

- **What were the characteristics of the pain? Can your client describe what he experienced?**

- **What was the final diagnosis?**

- **Was any workup done? When? By whom? Which tests were performed? What was the client told about the results of those tests?**

- **What treatment was given? Was the client prescribed medication? Was he advised to have further tests? Surgery? What other advice was given by the physician who was seen for the chest pain(s)?**

Underwriting chest pain episodes is difficult. The first thing the underwriter considers is the likelihood of CAD being present, based upon the client's age, sex and coronary risk factor profile. A chest pain episode in a nonsmoking, premenopausal woman who does not have a long history of taking oral contraceptives is very unlikely to be due to CAD, no matter how suspicious the symptoms. Conversely, even seemingly innocent chest pains in a 60 year-old, cigarette smoking male with high cholesterol and/or hypertension must be underwritten much more conservatively.

If CAD is suspected by the attending physician, diagnostic testing will be mandated in most cases. There are many tests that may be used and some of those have already been described in Chapter 5. The leading diagnostic tests for CAD include:

- **Treadmill stress test.**

- **Myocardial perfusion imaging (thallium, technetium).**

- **Exercise echocardiography.**

- **Ultrafast CT scan.**

- **Coronary angiography.**

Suffice it to say that the underwriter must relentlessly pursue the details of all such tests.

Once a diagnosis of CAD is established, or your client has had a myocardial infarction (and survived to find a renewed interest in life insurance!), the underwriting focus changes. Now, the underwriter needs to know three things:

1. **the type(s) of treatment(s) undertaken or advised. (Medication, surgery.)**

2. **The extent of anatomical disease. (Which arteries are obstructed, to what extent?)**

3. **How well does your client's heart work despite this disease? (Key factors include response to stress testing, left ventricular ejection fraction, irregularities of ventricular wall movement, blood flow defects on imaging, etc.)**

The bottom line: the more information the underwriter has, the better your chances of getting the best possible offer. Detailed reports from physicians and hospitals, replete with copies of all test reports, surgical summaries, etc., are ideal. Substandard brokerage pros know that the key to getting someone insured at a deliverable premium rate who has had a heart attack, bypass or coronary angioplasty, is to make sure the underwriter gets *more* information, not *less*.

CAD Risk Factor Analysis

With the advent of widespread use of lab testing in life underwriting, it became possible to perform fairly sophisticated coronary risk factor analysis. In addition to knowing the client's age, sex, family history, blood pressure and build, the underwriter now had access to multiple CAD risk-related variables on blood (lipids, diabetic markers) and urine (cotinine, microalbumin) test reports.

Coronary risk factor analysis is an important part of life underwriting. Desirable profiles are not only associated with a greatly reduced risk of developing clinical coronary artery disease, they also argue for favorable, overall mortality, relative to someone with an average or, frankly, undesirable profile. Thus, coronary risk profile components play a dominant role in how underwriters decide who is (and who is not) a "preferred" or "superpreferred" risk.

The three cardinal CAD risk factors are said to be:

1. **high blood pressure (hypertension);**

2. **high total cholesterol; and**

3. **cigarette smoking.**

Current data on all three are available on all paramedically or medically examined risks requiring a blood profile.

Before we examine the significance of these three major risk factors, three other risk factors should be mentioned briefly. They are important but also immutable, which is to say they cannot be influenced by any intervention.

1. **Age. Although lesions destined to represent coronary artery disease have been discovered in teenagers (during an autopsy), CAD is primarily a disease of aging. The older the applicant, the higher the risk.**

2. **Sex.** Not how often—but which one! Men are more prone than women to earlier development of CAD. Clinically evident CAD is distinctly rare in premenopausal females.

3. **Family history.** There is a significant familial component in one's risk of developing CAD. This relates to both inherited and behavioral (lifestyle) factors. Underwriters look unfavorably on premature (that is, occurring under age 60 in males and under age 70 in females) coronary events/deaths in parents and siblings.

High blood pressure, high cholesterol and cigarette smoking are acclaimed as the three major CAD risk factors. The database supporting their status is impressive.

High Blood Pressure

Although there are no statistics, it is logical to assume that elevated blood pressure is a leading cause of adverse medical underwriting action on life insurance applications. Underwriters usually consider 140 systolic and 90 diastolic to be the upper limits of "normal" because there is extensive data linking higher blood pressure levels to significant extra mortality.

Hypertension is insidious. Its lethal effects develop gradually over decades. Individuals with longstanding hypertension often have left ventricular hypertrophy (LVH), which is itself an ominous cardiac risk factor. They also lose protein due to hypertensive kidney damage, resulting in proteinuria and/ or microalbuminuria. Underwriters screen for this with urine specimens.

Most underwriting manuals provide detailed algorithms for interfacing current blood pressure readings, recorded during the paramedical, with historic readings taken from physicians' reports. A weighted averaging system is typical. Further adjustments are made for antihypertensive treatment, thus assuring maximum recognition of effective blood pressure control. Additional debits may be added for complications (proteinuria/microalbuminuria, LVH, etc.). Increasingly, such algorithms allow credits as well. If the client has a long history of well-controlled hypertension and is known to be free of complications, the final rating may be adjusted downward; perhaps there will be no rating at all.

Considering hypertension's implied status as a major source of ratings, be mindful of the advice given in Chapter 4. The client should present himself for the exam in a manner that minimizes the risk of elevated readings. Make sure the examiner follows the instructions on the exam form; it might call for additional readings if the first is elevated. Under that circumstance, additional readings should *always* be performed because temporary elevations attributable to anxiety at the start of an exam will tend to normalize as time passes. It is also advantageous for the client's physician to include blood pressure readings from his charts when he responds to the APS request. A pattern of normal readings can help minimize the impact of high, first time readings on a paramedical.

Blood Lipids

Four lipids are routinely measured both on insurance and clinical blood profiles:

1. **total cholesterol;**

2. **high density (HDL-C) cholesterol;**

3. **low density (LDL-C) cholesterol; and**

4. **triglycerides.**

With the exception of HDL-C, elevated levels correlate with increased risk. Since HDL is recognized as "good" cholesterol, HDL-C levels are inverse to the risk of developing CAD. In general, the higher one's HDL-C, the lower the risk of CAD.

When lipids are elevated, physicians will usually try to lower them with medication, lifestyle and dietary changes. The exception, of course, is the HDL-C that they will try to raise, if it is too low, by the same interventions.

Since lipid levels are only partially under dietary control, individuals with more severe lipid abnormalities will likely be given medication. Many lipid-modifying drugs are now available and some are widely prescribed. These drugs include six so-called reductase inhibitors or "statins" such as lovastatin (Mevacor), simvistatin (Zocor), gemfibrozil (Lopid) and niacin.

Unlike the others, niacin can be purchased over-the-counter without a prescription. It has, though, a number of side effects that include possible liver enzyme elevations. Individuals taking niacin (or *any other* physician prescribed or self-prescribed medication) should always acknowledge the fact on the Part II.

Cigarette Smoking

Nicotine is a heart stimulant as well as a potent vasoconstrictor capable of causing arteries to suddenly narrow. Cigarette smoke is loaded with carbon monoxide which inhibits oxygen utilization. These adverse effects are major promoters of myocardial ischemic events.

Since these effects are mainly acute, the good news is that when one quits cigarette smoking, there are immediate benefits. In longtime smokers, an increased risk of tobacco-related cancer persists for years, even decades, after quitting. Conversely, cardiovascular health benefits accrue almost immediately.

Diabetes Mellitus

Diabetes is a major risk factor for all three major presentations of atherosclerotic disease: CAD; cerebrovascular disease; and peripheral arterial disease. The same is true for anyone with chronic high blood sugar (hyperglycemia) in the absence of a definite diagnosis of diabetes.

In many cases, individuals with persistently abnormal blood sugars who do not (yet) meet the criteria for being called diabetic, are said to have "impaired glucose tolerance" (IGT) or "impaired fasting glucose" (IFG). Those are significant CAD risk factors, whether or not actual diabetes has been diagnosed.

Build

Overweight/obesity is widely recognized as a risk factor for CAD, mostly through its "guilt by association" link to elevated blood lipids, high blood pressure and chronic hyperglycemia/diabetes.

New Risk Factors

Many potential CAD risk factors have been identified by medical researchers in recent years. Some of those factors include high levels of the lipid marker lipoproetin Lp(a), the protein homocysteine and the blood clotting protein fibrinogen. Also, elevation of a test for chronic inflammation known as c-reactive protein (CRP), nonuse (vs. use) of hormone replacement therapy (HRT) by postmenopausal females and a history of chronic depression. As more is known about the significance of these new risk factors, some will undoubtedly find their way into CAD risk factor profiling for underwriting purposes.

Build

There is no doubt that overweight/obesity, as reflected in "build" (weight in relation to height), is a leading cause of adverse action in life underwriting. A great wealth of insurance data has been accumulated over the years relating mortality to build. That is a reason why build tables are used as a basis for deciding who is overweight.

Statistics reveal an interesting phenomenon. Mortality related to build tends to be "J" shaped. The "J" refers to the slope of the mortality curve on a two dimensional graph where the horizontal axis shows build and the vertical axis shows death rates.

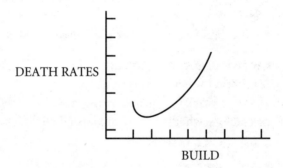

DEATH RATES

BUILD

The "J" shape to this mortality curve indicates there is excess mortality associated with both underweight and significantly overweight individuals. Nonetheless, an extremely underweight person is not a common problem in North America and most build-related, adverse underwirting actions are taken because of overweight.

Height and weight are measured during paramedicals and full medical exams. A person's weight is recorded while he is wearing normal clothing. If the client has experienced a recent weight loss, that is also recorded, along with the reason for and the extent of that weight loss. It is very important for the client to report if he was/is actively engaged in some type of weight loss program related to the said weight loss.

Ratings for overweight individuals are usually subject to reconsideration if the client loses a significant amount of weight *and maintains that weight loss for a stipulated period of time.* The latter is an essential criterion because, unfortunately, most weight that is lost is once again found, often with a few bonus pounds!

Build (weight in relation to height) is one of several ways of deciding who is overweight/obese and who is not. Yet, it might not be the ideal way. There is a growing body of data to suggest that, at least in the cases of individuals who are mild-to-moderately overweight, build might not be the key to the nature of the risk. It might matter less *if* you have some excess weight than *where* that weight is carried!

Clinical medicine makes use of a number of so-called anthropomorphic indices. These are refinements in the way being overweight is measured. There are two main indices:

1. **body mass index (BMI); and**

2. **waist-to-hip ratio.**

Body mass index is determined by a simple formula which relates weight to height. Waist-to-hip ratio is, literally, the ratio of the circumference of the waist to that of the hips. This ratio is easily measured.

Researchers have found that adipose tissue (fat) carried in the abdominal region, sometimes called android obesity or abdominal obesity, is metabolically undesirable. It is linked to elevated lipids, hypertension and high blood sugar levels. Conversely, adiposity carried mainly in the hips, thighs and buttocks appears to be much less detrimental. Thus, individuals with a high waist-to-hip ratio might represent the subset of more adverse "overweight" risks.

Waist-to-hip ratios are not yet being measured routinely during paramedical examinations; perhaps they should be.

Cerebrovascular and Peripheral Arterial Disease

Coronary artery disease is the most common form of atherosclerotic disease seen in insurance applicants. The other two major forms affect the arteries carrying blood to the brain (cerebrovascular disease) and to the lower extremities (peripheral arterial disease), respectively.

The two major manifestations of cerebrovascular disease are stroke (cerebrovascular accident or CVA) and transient ischemic attack (TIA). When applicants have a history of stroke or TIA, underwriting is very meticulous and is focused on medical records. The producer best expedites those cases by facilitating the timely release of detailed medical records, *including copies of all diagnostic test reports.* The more information the underwriter has, the better the chance of a favorable decision.

Many TIAs and even some strokes in persons under age 50 will be due to causes other than cerebral artery atherosclerosis. In some of those cases, the risk of a second event might be minimal and such cases can often be underwritten favorably after a period of time. Once again, the key is to facilitate the release of *complete* medical records.

Peripheral arterial disease of the lower extremities is usually due to atherosclerosis and is seen mainly in older (over age 60) applicants. Diabetics and cigarette smokers are prone to develop this disease much earlier in life than nondiabetics/nonsmokers. They also tend to have a more severe disease, a fact best underscored by the high rates of lower extremity amputation (the final treatment option) in diabetics and unreformed smokers.

The cardinal presenting symptom in peripheral arterial disease is called intermittent claudication. Simply stated, this is pain in the buttocks, thigh or calf muscle brought on by exertion and relieved by rest. The client may simply say that he gets cramps or a "charley horse" when he walks the golf course and has, thus, opted for an electric cart for future rounds of golf. Such a history could well represent intermittent claudication.

In underwriting peripheral arterial disease, the emphasis is placed on the medical history. Once again, it is to the agent's advantage to have *detailed* records, with complete reports of all tests and surgeries, expedited to the underwriter. The more information the underwriter has, the better the chance of a favorable decision. The converse is also true. Incomplete records with key details absent, as well as scenarios where the client does not comply with the physician's advice regarding testing and/or treatment, are associated with less favorable underwriting outcomes. How could it be otherwise?

One relatively simple test, known as the ankle-to-arm (or, ankle:briachial) blood pressure index, is particularly instructive whenever signs or symptoms suggest peripheral arterial disease. When individuals have lower blood pressure in the legs than in the arms, this suggests significant amounts of atherosclerotic blockage can be present.

Heart Murmurs

The incidence of significant heart murmurs seen by underwriters has declined greatly in recent years. This is mainly due to advances in the treatment of acute rheumatic fever (a major source of heart valve damage) and to improved diagnostic tests (echocardiograms) for distinguishing pathologic murmurs from their innocent counetrparts.

Heart murmurs due to cardiac disease are typically called "organic." In most cases, they involve either the aortic valve and/or the mitral valve, which both serve the heart's main pumping chamber, the left ventricle. Murmurs indicative of possible damage to any of the four heart valves are evaluated both by auscultation (listening to the heart with a stethoscope) and by echocardiogram (a painless test in which sound waves are used to create a "picture" of the heart).

Echocardiograms are too expensive to be ordered as regular underwriting requirements. However, they are routinely used in clinical diagnosis so most patients with a heart murmur history will also have one or more echocardiogram reports in their records. Seeing the details of the cardiology assessment, and especially the report of the echocardiogram, is essential to getting the most favorable assessment of any heart murmur.

There are three relatively common disorders that give rise to heart murmurs:

1. **Bicuspid aortic valve. The individual is born with an aortic valve that has two leaflets (cusps) instead of the normal three. This abnormal valve architecture is predisposed to developing calcifications by mid-life. That, in turn, can lead, in time, to a leaky (regurgitant, insufficient) or narrowed (stenotic) valve. Some individuals will need valve replacement surgery.**

2. **Mitral valve prolapse (MVP). This is probably the most common "heart murmur" scenario seen by underwriters. In MVP, the leaflets of the mitral valve, located between the left atrium and left ventricle of the heart, move abnormally during the systolic phase of the cardiac cycle, often producing distinctive heart sounds. Although there are a number of potential causes, MVP is almost always a benign condition that has little, if any, mortality impact. The echocardiogram is the key to the proper identification and analysis of MVP.**

3. **Hypertrophic cardiomyopathy (HCM). Some people are genetically predisposed to developing insidious thickening of the wall in the heart that separates the ventricles. This wall,**

known as the intraventricular septum, can become so thick that it interferes with the flow of blood through the aortic valve opening as the heart pumps. When that happens, the victim may have symptoms such as chest pain, loss of consciousness and heart rhythm disturbances. Hypertrophic cardiomyopathy is much less common than bicuspid aortic valve or mitral valve prolapse, but the incidence of its discovery is rising, especially in older applicants. The key to identifying this impairment, as in the case of MVP, is the echocardiogram.

Diabetes Mellitus

There are three basic types of diabetes:

1. type 1;

2. type 2; and

3. gestational.

Although all three share the common problem of high blood sugar levels, they present different degrees of risk from an underwriting perspective.

Gestational diabetes, named for the fact that it arises during pregnancy, is (usually) a temporary condition that remits after childbirth. Women who develop gestational diabetes during pregnancy have an increased risk of becoming type 2 diabetics later in life.

Type 1, which was formerly known as insulin-dependent diabetes, accounts for roughly 10 percent of diabetic diagnoses in North America. Onset is typically before age 35 and the patient invaribaly requires insulin injections to avoid life-threatening complications.

What was called non-insulin-dependent diabetes is now known simply as type 2. It is, by far, the most common diabetic state encountered by underwriters. Unlike type 1 patients who are often diagnosed after experiencing symptoms, the typical type 2 diabetic is first suspected of having this impaiment when a routine screening blood profile discloses an elevated blood sugar level.

Many type 2 diabetics are symptom-free and the major threat to their health is their enhanced risk of developing atherosclerotic disease (CAD, etc.). Diabetic kidney, eye and nervous system complications occur often in type 2 diabetics, but their overall prevalence is much lower than in type 1 diabetes.

Many type 2 diabetics can be effectively managed with weight loss, dietary modifications and oral medications; others require insulin injections. The overriding consideration is that they achieve the best possible control of their blood sugar levels. It is now clear, from a landmark study completed in the early 1990s, that chronically elevated blood sugar is the key to most diabetic complications.

In both major forms of diabetes mellitus, underwriting is related to three main factors:

1. **duration of the disease;**

2. **degree of control of the blood sugar; and**

3. **the presence, or absence, of key complications.**

The emphasis on duration relates to the fact that, in general, the longer the individual has been diabetic, the higher the probability that insidious kidney and circulatory complications will be present.

Underwriters evaluate diabetic control in two ways. They request physicians' records because those should provide a track record of periodic examinations which, in turn, will show blood and urine glucose, glycosylated hemoglobin and microalbumin test results (refer to Chapter 5 for more details on these tests).

Underwriters also rely on current lab testing. This may include both blood (glucose, glycosylated hemoglobin, fructosamine) and urine (glucose, microalbumin) testing. If current test results are desirable, the prospect for a favorable underwriting outcome rises considerably.

When an applicant has an elevated blood sugar, suggesting an increased risk of diabetes, the underwriter may require both additional blood tests and a urine specimen. That works to the client's advantage. If the tests are normal, the odds of a favorable underwriting decision increase. On the other hand, if abnormalities are found, further workup by the client's physician might detect diabetes at any early stage. Through careful blood sugar control and other clinical interventions, the prognosis can be greatly improved. Thus, early discovery of an unsuspected diabetic condition can have important ramifications for the quality (and quantity) of the client's life as well as for his ultimate insurability.

The CAD risk profile of a diabetic applicant is a major factor in determining his insurability. Hypertension, hyperlipidemia, obesity, cigarette smoking and other major risk factors take on added significance in diabetics. The synergy of their impact might translate to a high rating or even a refusal to accept the risk. Conversely, a complication free diabetic with an otherwise highly favorable CAD risk profile epitomizes what underwriters are fond of calling a "best case."

Cancer

Malignant tumors are the second leading cause of death after coronary artery disease. Due to the progress made in screening for CAD in insurance applicants, cancer is often found to be the *leading* cause of early death claims.

"Cancer" is a generic term derived from the Greek word for crab. It is used to describe what are, in reality, over two hundred disease processes that have one thing in common. They are all characterized by unrestrained growths of abnormal cells capable, if unchecked by the host's own defensives or by medical intervention, of killing that host.

These unrestrained growths (malignant tumors) can spread from the original (primary) site where the cancer first developed. The term for that process is "metastasis." In general, the fact that a cancer has metastasized greatly reduces the likelihood that it will be cured or insured. There are, however, noteworthy exceptions to this "rule" such as Hodgkin's disease, certain pediatric malignancies and cancers of the testicle.

The underwriting of cancer usually involves the use of temporary, flat extra premiums, expressed in dollar amounts per thousand for a fixed interval (for example, $10 per thousand for six years). The rationale for this is that most cancer victims who succumb will do so in a relatively short interval (typically 5 to 10 years, sometimes longer), measured from when the tumor is diagnosed and treated.

In most but not all forms of cancer, patients who survive ten years without recurrence have only a small risk that the tumor will subsequently reappear and prove fatal. There are notable exceptions to this rule, too. The complexity of cancer underwriting is perhaps best exemplified by the fact that one of us (HG) once wrote a cancer underwriting manual more than 300 pages long!

Cancer underwriting is meticulous. It is also highly dependent upon information from the attending physician, as well as all other physicians involved in the cancer care of the proposed insured. The three most critical components to underwriting analysis are:

1. The pathology report(s). This is the source for establishing the *precise* diagnosis and it also plays a key role in assessing the prognosis. For example, there are five major kinds of thyroid cancer. One is rarely fatal; one almost invariably kills; the others fall between these prognostic extremes. The way to determine which one was present is to read the *full* pathology report *with great care*.

2. The details of diagnosis and treatment. The most critical document is (usually) the discharge summary from the hospital where the diagnostic workup was done, the stage of the cancer was determined and the treatment that was given.

3. Full details of every interim medical history, especially the follow-up tests that could detect relapses/recurrences as well as evidence of any late complications due to the therapy. Cancer treatments, such as radiation and chemotherapeutic drugs, can, themselves, be potentially life-threatening. It is, unfortunately, not rare for someone to be cured of a cancer but, instead, develop complications, including, possibly, even a second malignant tumor, from their curative treatment. Underwriters will be mindful of every detail of a cancer history. Turnaround time on cancer cases must always be subordinated to a thorough and complete underwriting analysis.

An applicant with a history of cancer is aware he has had (in most cases) a life-threatening illness. You will encounter less resistance to delays in underwriting from such individuals as they will be focused on the final decision. You are best served by doing whatever you can to facilitate the requirements. In some cases, these can include two, three or even four physician/hospital APS reports. The more information in those reports, the better the chance of a favorable outcome. Faced with gaps in medical information, the underwriter will be very conservative with most cancer cases. Mistakes will often prove to be claims.

Psychiatric Impairments

Psychiatric disorders are among the most difficult impairments to underwrite. The main problem relates directly to acquiring adequate information with which to assess the risk. Remember, when the underwriter does not have enough information, when the history is vague or ambiguous, or when the underwriter must rely on inferences rather than facts, his decision must be conservative.

The leading cause of early death claims on cases with a psychiatric history is suicide, another is accidents. Experts believe a significant share of suicides are officially recorded as accidental deaths. The incidence of suicide is particularly high in major psychiatric impairments such as major depressive disorder, bipolar (manic-depressive) disorder, shcizophrenia and other psychoses, substance abuse and, some would argue, panic disorder. Our ability to underwrite these impairments for the suicide/accident risk is very limited.

Psychiatric disorders are chronic conditions; relapse is the rule rather than the exception. Some individuals do not respond to any therapy; others relapse again and again despite treatment. Many of the major psychiatric impairments have significant extra mortality—nearly all of them represent a formidable morbidity risk.

How can the producer help expedite such cases? Once again, the more information the underwriter has, the more details he can review regarding the signs and symptoms, diagnosis, course of the illnesses (duration since the last symptoms, number of relapses, complications), type(s) of therapy given/currently taken, etc., and the more likely it is that the decision will be as favorable as possible.

On business submitted non-medically, make sure you take an adequate history. If there is not sufficient space on the Part II to record all the details volunteered by the client, attach an additional sheet (signed and dated by the client as well as yourself). The more information from the client's perspective, the better.

Attending physicians' statements from psychiatric practitioners (as well as those from other physicians reporting on psychiatric case histories) are distinguished by their brevity. Unfortunately, psychiatric impairments are thought by many people to confer some sort of stigma or guilt (as if having bipolar disorder, for example, was indicative of a character defect!). As evidence continues to link these illnesses to biological disturbances in the release and re-uptake of neurotransmitter chemicals in the brain, psychiatric impairments will, hopefully, become more and more destigmatized. In the meantime, underwriting those risks is impeded by terse APS reports and uninformative histories offered up by apprehensive insurance seekers.

If your client has contact with his psychiatric caregiver regarding the request for underwriting information, it is appropriate for the client to urge that the report to the insurer be as complete as possible. What was the exact diagnosis?

When was the impairment diagnosed? How often have exacerbations or relapses occurred? How long has the client been relapse-free? What type(s) of treatment have been given, previously and currently? Have they been effective? Have there been any thoughts of or attempts at suicide? What effect has the impairment had on the client's employment and personal life? What is the caregiver's assessment of the prognosis? Those are the kinds of questions underwriters would like to see addressed in APS reports on psychiatric histories and by prospective insureds on the Part II or on accompanying statements.

Substance Abuse

The two major forms of substance abuse encountered by life underwriters are:

1. **alcohol abuse; and**

2. **the habitual use of certain (mainly illicit) drugs.**

These impairments are in the domain of psychiatric medicine. The diagnostic criteria for substance abuse disorders are delineated in the *Diagnostic and Statistical Manual (DSM IV)*, currently in its fourth edition, published by the American Psychiatric Association.

The underwriting problems presented by psychiatric impairments (noted above) are very similar to those encountered in cases involving a history of alcohol or drug abuse/dependence. Medical histories, both as reported by applicants and by their caregivers, tend to be scant. Records from treatment facilities are often difficult to obtain. Those factors might force underwriters to be more conservative.

Alcoholism and drug abuse can be devastating illnesses. Since the core problem is addiction, the risk of relapse is high. Significant psychiatric conditions are several times more prevalent among substances abusers than in the general population. The risk of suicide in both chronic alcoholism and in certain forms of drug abuse, especially cocaine addiction, is formidable. There are also a wide range of non-psychiatric impairments associated directly with alcohol abuse and most types of drug abuse.

For example, alcohol abuse is a leading cause of cirrhosis of the liver. This is an irreversible and often fatal disorder. Impairments arising in virtually every organ system are significantly prevalent among chronic alcohol abusers. Full details of the medical history, as well as current medical tests, are essential when underwriting an applicant with a history of alcohol abuse/alcoholism.

Since the risk of a relapse from all addictive disorders is highest in the first years after the attainment of sobriety (drug free status), there is an interval, measured from completion of treatment, when coverage is postponed. Thereafter, insurability is based upon both continued freedom from relapse *and* the absence of significant complications.

Underwriters seek out the full details of the medical history; inspection reports and motor vehicle records are routine. To repeat a theme that might now seem redundant, the more information the underwriter has, the more favorable the decision is likely to be.

The client can help his own cause in this regard.

- **Has he remained alcohol/drug free?**

- **Does he actively and regularly participate in Alcoholics Anonymous (AA) or an equivalent 12-step program?**

Those details belong on the Part II or in an accompanying statement taken over the insured's signature.

Substance abuse histories are volatile and associated with many causes of death. Do what you can to encourage full disclosure of the facts. Cover letters can be tremendously helpful in putting these challenging, multifactorial cases in some sort of underwriting perspective.

AIDS

The name AIDS, an acronym for acquired immunodeficiency syndrome, has been given to a chronic disorder said to be caused by human immunodeficiency viruses Type I (HIV-1) and Type 2 (HIV-2). Virtually all AIDS cases in North America are linked to HIV-1 infection.

AIDS is associated with a wide range of life-endangering complications including systemic infections, malignancies, dementia and intractable pathologies affecting many organs.

AIDS is now one of the leading causes of death in young adult males in the United States; it is also among the leading causes of death in young women.

Although the majority of confirmed cases are in certain "high risk" groups, this disorder has been spread, for example, from males with a history of intravenous drug abuse to their nondrug-abusing female sexual partners. Transmission of the HIV-1 virus by dentists to patients, from mothers to offspring and among needle-sharing anabolic steroid users has also been confirmed. For all those reasons, AIDS is a major concern to life, health and disability insurers.

Oral fluid and urine HIV tests represent a substanial (and growing) part of insurance AIDS testing. The results provided by those tests often result in faster underwriting approvals, especially where the agent is directly involved in collecting the specimen at the time of the application.

Hepatitis

Hepatitis means "inflammation of the liver." There are many forms of hepatitis, classified according to cause (viruses, alcohol, etc.). Most potentially insurable hepatitis cases seen by underwriters will involve viral hepatitis. There are five basic varieties of clincally evident viral hepatitis, designated as hepatitis A, B, C, D and E respectively. Two of those (hepatitis D and E) are seldom seen among North American insurance buyers.

Hepatitis A (HAV) presents little, if any, underwriting problem. Once the diagnosis is established by blood testing and the patient has recovered, life and disability insurance coverage is available in nearly every case. Acute hepatitis A never gives rise to chronic hepatitis and has no carrier state.

Hepatitis B (HBV) is much less common in North America than in other parts of the world. In large areas of Asia, it is a major cause of morbidity and mortality. As HBV is so prevalent in much of Asia, the incidence of chronic hepatitis B infection, as well as the hepatitis B carrier state, is greatly increased among persons who emigrated to North America from those parts of Asia.

In North America, hepatitis B is also a major sexually transmitted disease but it can be acquired in other ways as well.

Many individuals, when initially infected with HBV, do not develop an apparent acute illness; some will have no symptoms whatsoever. Mortality associated with *acute* hepatitis B is minimal. The problem is, some acutely infected individuals will develop chronic hepatitis B or become silent HBV carriers.

Chronic hepatitis B can be mild and nonprogressive, or it can lead to cirrhosis and liver carcinoma. It is usually unclear at the time of underwriting (even if the proposed insured has had a liver biopsy) whether or not the individual will eventaully develop life-endangering complications. This augers for conservative undewriting.

When a person is infected with the hepatitis B virus, the test for the hepatitis B surface antigen (HBsAg) will be positive. This is a relatively inexpensive blood test and it is the most commonly used hepatitis B test in life underwriting.

If an individual tests positive for HBsAg, a second test, known as the "e" antigen test (HBeAg), can sometimes help determine if he has active, ongoing liver inflammation. For that reason, underwriters ask insurance labs to perform the "e" antigen test on most applicants who test positive for the hepatitis B virus.

Individuals infected with the virus (HBsAg+), who test negative for the "e" antigen, who have no signs or symptoms of liver disease and who have normal liver enzymes, are usually said to be hepaitis B carriers. That means they harbor the virus. Even though most carriers are currently well, they are at risk for future adverse activity by the virus they carry which means they might eventually develop cirrhosis and/or liver cancer. So long as HBV remains in their body, they require lifelong follow-ups by their physician and careful scrutiny in the underwriting process.

Hepatitis C (HCV) is another story altogether. Like hepatitis B, it can become a chronic illness. Unlike HBV (where most acutely infected patients recover completely), experts believe that at least 80 percent of individuals who contract hepatitis C will progress, in time, to the chronic form of the illness. Those who do are at risk for cirrhosis and liver cancer. However, it is very difficult, with hepatitis C, to say which cases will progress to life-endangering sequelae. Thus, the underwriting of chronic hepatitis C tends to be both thorough and very conservative.

If your client acknowledges a history of hepatitis, try to clarify which type of hepatitis he had. That is very important and needs to be communicated on the Part II. With the exception of confirmed hepatitis A, expect that the underwriter will require an APS and current blood tests.

If your client has had a liver biopsy, the underwriter will insist on seeing a report from the physician who ordered the biopsy and, above all, a copy of the pathology report. If your client is said to be a hepatitis B or C carrier, the underwriter will need to see the results of his hepatitis tests as well as all liver function tests, etc.

The main treatments for chronic HBV and HCV are medication (interferon-alfa and other drugs) and surgery (liver transplantation). There are no rules of thumb on these cases. The underwriter needs all of the details of the history, with particular emphasis on those related to the interval since completion of the treatment. The majority of cases will probably be uninsurable. It is hoped that this will change as more and more medically and surgically treated chronic hepatitis B and C patients survive longer and longer without complications or late relapses.

Tobacco and Risk Selection

In 1964, the U.S. Surgeon General issued his epistle on the adverse health consequences of smoking. A decade and a half later, life insurance companies had accumulated sufficient data on the mortality associated with cigarette smoking to take the historic step of offering "smoker" vs. "nonsmoker" premium rates.

"Smoker" was defined, in those early days, as someone who smoked cigarettes, in most cases, within twelve months of applying for insurance. "Smokers" paid higher premiums; non-cigarette smoking tobacco users were accorded "non-smoker" status.

Fifteen years after the introduction of cigarettes-only "smoker" premiums, insurers began to change their definition of tobacco use. Today, the most prevalent definition of a "user" includes anyone who has used tobacco in any form, including oral (snuff, chewing tobacco), as well as anyone consuming nicotine in any form. The latter involves nicotine therapies (the patch, gum, etc.) used, in the vast majority of cases, by persons trying to wean themselves from tobacco use.

There are several key reasons for changing from "cigarettes only" to "all forms of tobacco" or "any nicotine use." First, any type of regular tobacco use is associated with excess mortality and morbidity. Tobacco, smoked or chewed, inhaled or not, is a major carcinogen. Second, individuals using nicotine replacement in the form of the gum or the patch are, unfortunately, at a very high risk for relapse to their original delivery system.

A second reason for adopting a tobacco-wide definition of "smoker" has to do with our credibility as an industry. There is no doubt (among those who are objective) that tobacco use is highly addictive, that it is fraught with health consequences for chronic users (not to mention "passive smokers" forced to breath family members' and co-workers' smoke) and that the decision to use tobacco is voluntary. True, users may desire to quit and fail to succeed when they try, but the fact remains that no one is held down and forced to smoke against his will!

The decision to use tobacco is voluntary—it is a health habit choice. If insurers do not recognize that and reflect it in insurance pricing, they lose credibility. It is hard to explain to consumers why we charge people who have had a heart attack higher premiums than those who have not if, at the same time, we did not do likewise with people who opt to increase their mortality and morbidity risks through the *voluntary* use of tobacco. The same could be said of people who drive drunk or engage in hazardous avocations.

Unfortunately, a significant percentage of individuals who use tobacco show evidence of a transient amnestic condition we call "smoker's amnesia" when they seek insurance coverage. This malady strikes at all-too-predictable times (fact finding interviews, at the completion of the application and personal history interviews).

Simply stated, if 5 percent of tobacco users with "smoker's amnesia" succeeded in getting misclassified as "non-users," their subsequent adverse mortality/morbidity experience would undermine the pricing of "non-user" classes of business. That is manifestly unfair to the true non-users in those classes.

The industry has developed an antidote to "smoker's amnesia." It is called a "nicotine" (actually, cotinine) test. That subject was fully discussed in Chapter 5.

Insurers take tobacco use very seriously. If an individual opts to misrepresent his tobacco use proclivities and if that misrepresentation is discovered by the insurer at a time when there is an available legal remedy (reformation, rescission or denial of a claim), assume that the appropriate remedy will be accessed. The courts have agreed with the argument that tobacco use is material.

Some have advanced the argument that if the insured has misrepresented his smoking status and then had a claim during the contestable period, the insurer should be compelled to pay a benefit which is proportional to the amount of coverage that could have been purchased by that same individual, for the same premium, at "smoker" rates. This argument has now largely been rejected.

Prospective life and disability insurance buyers need to understand that if they misrepresent their true tobacco use at the time of the application and if the insurance is issued and placed in force on a "non-smoker" or "non-user" basis, they are at risk for those legal remedies. Their "death benefit" might become little more than the sum of the premiums they have paid!

Genetic Information and Adverse Selection

Your genes affect virtually every aspect of your body's functions and your lifelong health. Even the impact of external injuries on your health is influenced by your genetic code. The predictive value of genetic information depends upon many factors beyond the scope of this chapter and book.

Put simply, some people are born "presymptomatic" for disease or disorders. The only question is, when will they become symptomatic? Other people might be born with a "predisposition" to develop a disease or disorder. Yet, whether they do or not is dependent upon environmental and/or behavioral factors.

Life insurers use a person's history of symptoms combined with existing states of health or latency, as measured by medical exams and tests of current function, to appraise mortality risk. The risk classification system incorporates insured lives experience with clinical research results and well-established medical knowledge. The integrity of underwriting is only as good as the integrity of the medical history provided by the applicant in combination with the examination and functional test results.

If the integrity of the medical history is invalid because of misrepresentation, the adequacy of the premium charged is also invalid. On a large scale, this state of adverse selection by applicants against insurance companies would undermine the financial strength of insurers and impair public perceptions of the fairness of the premiums insurers charge for life insurance.

There is public concern about insurer access to genetic medical information, let alone against genetic screening of insurance applicants. The life insurance industry does not intentionally seek to expand its insurance testing practices to include genetic screens. However, insurers must know as much about an applicant's medical status as the applicant does in order to properly classify risks and to establish adequate premiums. This is consistent with insurers' fiduciary obligations to their existing policyholders.

Many legislative proposals have been made to prohibit insurer access to genetic information about applicants. The key problem in most proposals centers on the definition of "genetic information." If the definition is kept very narrow and restricted to "results of direct tests of DNA, RNA or chromosomes," then insurers will still be able to evaluate the common biochemical tests of today. If insurer access to genetic information, especially if defined broadly (i.e., encompassing such tests as cholesterol levels, blood pressure or even height and weight), were legally prohibited, the following survival strategies and consequences would be likely:

- **Premiums would rise and interest in life insurance products by healthy persons would drop.**

- **Agent commissions would be reduced to maintain competitiveness in marketplace pricing.**

- **Small and medium-sized insurance companies would be forced to merge with large companies to maintain financial strength and their obligations to policyholders, thereby reducing the availability and affordability of life insurance in the general marketplace.**

- **Individual disability insurance would eventually disappear and be replaced by high premium, non-guaranteed renewable group and association products.**

Clinical genetic testing by health care providers is expanding. Insurers are keeping abreast of developments and developing risk classifications for the proper pricing of mortality risks identified in the clinical setting. The same rigid criteria applied to other medical information, such as sensitivity and specificity of medical test results, will be applied to genetic information. Premiums will be based on sound actuarial principles and reasonably anticipated experience. This will be no different than the standards for risk-based insurance pricing today.

Your ability to explain this issue in easy-to-understand terms for your clients is not only important to your financial future, it is important to their financial future.

CHAPTER 7

Medical Underwriting: Additional Issues

Repeat Testing and Rechecks

There are a limited number of medical underwriting scenarios where underwriters will seek to repeat medical tests. In other situations, you may feel the need to appeal for additional testing in order to assuage your concerns or those raised by your client.

The practice of routinely reexamining blood pressure is becoming less and less common. The two biggest reasons for that are expense control and the desire to get the policy approved on a timely basis. Obviously, there are advantages to having additional readings, especially if the first set of readings is out of pattern with the client's medical history.

Underwriters frequently call for a repeat urinalysis when proteinuria is present. In some companies, two additional specimens may be requested, with the quantities of protein in those specimens averaged. If protein is present only in the original specimen and the additional specimen(s) is/are free of further protein, favorable underwriting action is likely in many cases.

It is to the client's advantage to make sure that rechecks are completed in the manner requested and on a timely basis. Remember, whenever the underwriter initiates a request for any type of recheck, the odds are that the underwriting outcome will be *more favorable* with the rechecks than without them.

In some underwriting environments, there might be established practices related to rechecks involving other medical tests, such as elevations of blood lipids, liver enzymes, PSA, etc. Once again, the same logic applies. If a recheck is requested, the first test was, by inference, abnormal. There might also be other scenarios where a recheck is requested, such as when the first specimen was technically inadequate for analysis due to the manner in which it was collected or for some other reason.

Post-Underwriting Notification

If adverse underwriting action is taken, the underwriter will communicate that to the producer in some fashion; company practices and procedures vary. This discussion is not intended to recommend or endorse any one practice or procedure in that regard. Rather, it will provide a general overview of common industry practices and their implications for the producer and his client.

The client may become concerned when he learns that he is not being offered insurance on the basis as applied for (i.e., "standard" or "preferred"). He may object to the fact that he is not considered to be as good a risk as he thought himself to be, or he may focus on the specific reason for the adverse action, expressing doubts as to its accuracy or validity. No matter what the client's motivations, the producer is put in a difficult position. He must act both in the best interests of his client and of his company.

Medical underwriting information is treated as confidential as outlined in Chapter 4. Therefore, there is a certain protocol followed for having information related to an underwriting decision released to the client. In most cases, the underwriter will ask for a signed and dated authorization from the client empowering the insurer to release medical information that has a bearing on the decision to the client's physician. The reason the information is preferentially sent to the client's physician and not to the client himself is because most insurance buyers are lay people. They do not have the training necessary to fully interpret the test results and, thus, to understand the medical basis for the underwriting action. By providing the information to their physician, the expectation that the information is fully understood increases considerably (i.e., the doctor gets the information from the underwriter, contacts the client/patient and discusses the information with him).

This feedback loop has advantages. In addition to a better understanding as to why adverse action was taken, the client will get the benefit of a current medical appraisal of his situation. This might mean reinforcement of the need to take prescribed medication, etc. If there were current abnormal test findings that led to the decision, the physician may elect to repeat those tests and/or to perform additional tests. Sometimes, this process leads to the discovery of a significant impairment which the physician is then able to treat for the well-being of his patient.

If the client is upset and/or if the physician himself takes exception to the basis for the adverse underwriting decision, the decision can be appealed. That appeal can take various forms. In such scenarios, it is imperative that all parties keep in mind the significant differences between clinical medicine and insurance underwriting. Those differences are discussed later in this chapter.

In cases where adverse action is taken on the basis of very sensitive findings (positive drug test, positive HIV test), special handling procedures will likely be in place. Some of these practices may be mandated by regulatory authorities. Suffice it to say that, in sensitive cases such as those, the established protocol will be followed to the letter; it must be for the protection of your client.

Medical Reconsideration

If the insured accepts a policy rated for a medical reason, he may be eligible for future reconsideration of that rating. If your client is declined there might be circumstances under which that decision would also be reviewed. In both cases, you need to know the facts so you can properly advise your client.

Reconsideration of medical ratings is not always possible. For example, temporary, flat extra premiums for impairments like cancer drop off automatically. Some impairments, by their nature, are unlikely to improve enough to make the risk more favorable at any future interval. An example is diabetes. At this writing, there is no cure for this common disease. One of the key factors on which diabetic underwriting is based is the duration that the insured has been diabetic; the longer the duration, the greater the risk of complications and the higher the rating. Thus, there is little potential for reducing diabetic ratings in subsequent years. The same is true for many heart murmurs and certain other impairments as well.

The good news is that most common medical reasons for assessing a table rating are amenable to future reconsideration. This is important to the producer because knowing that the rating can be reduced, perhaps even removed (but never increased!) in the future, might encourage the client to accept a rated policy.

Whenever your client is rated or declined, ask about reconsideration. If you are told that reconsideration is possible at some future time, ask for clarification.

- **When?**
- **With what interim medical evidence?**

The answer to these questions depends entirely upon the impairment and your client's specific history. For example, a rating for elevated blood pressure may be reconsidered in one or two years. This is especially approriate if there has not been a long history of poorly controlled hypertension and complications have not already manifested themselves.

The major criterion for reconsideration of a blood pressure rating can be that the client has a stated number of interim blood pressure rechecks that show improvement (i.e., lower readings than those that led to the rating). If the rating is for build, sustained weight loss may be required. You should get the answers to these questions from the underwriter because those answers will help you deliver the rated policy. They will give you a basis for following up with your client or for eventually making a current non-client (declined) into a future true client (insurable).

There is another caveat. Let's say that your client is rated for high cholesterol or for elevated blood pressure. Those are two of the cardinal risk factors for coronary artery disease. Let's also say that in the two interim years since your client accepted delivery of his policy that was rated Table 2 for elevated blood pressure, two things happened. First, he was diagnosed as having coronary artery disease and was placed on medication. Second, his blood pressure improved substantially. The latter technically makes him eligible for reconsideration. However, the diagnosis of coronary artery disease takes precedence. There is no basis for reducing or removing a Table 2 rating in this situation. The logic of this should be clear.

Medical Underwriting Appeals

In nearly all North American life companies, the final underwriting decision on every case is made by the underwriter, directly or in consultation with his peers or superiors. Advice may be sought from technical experts, such as medical directors, but accountability for the final decision rests, appropriately, with the underwriter.

There is almost certainly an underwriting referral system in place. Such a system may have mandatory face amount/degree of rating thresholds at which underwriters *must* get a second opinion/second signature from more senior colleagues. The underwriter may also make voluntary use of the referral system whenever he feels the need for a second opinion.

This referral system may or may not reach the head of the underwriting department. Increasingly, the trend is for the top person in the day-to-day referral pyramid to be an expert technical underwriter who, in turn, reports to the head of the department. The department head may be an administrative manager in some cases, with little or no experience in actual case underwriting.

When you feel the need to make an appeal on a case, it is wise to do so directly to the underwriter who made the original decision. Decision-making accountability rests with that underwriter. His consultants (medical directors, etc.) and his superiors will look to him to respond to your appeal and to justify, or to change, his decision, based upon the merit of the information you offer in your appeal.

There is another factor to bear in mind. One case seldom makes or breaks a producer's career. Nevertheless, one unpleasant, negatively polarizing experience between a producer and an underwriter can set a tone for future dealings.

As a life insurance sales professional, you would be chagrined if your client went to your general agent or agency manager for a second opinion on the appropriateness of the coverage you recommended to him! Put yourself in the underwriter's position. If you truly believe you must appeal beyond the original underwriter, do so with his blessing or at least his acknowledgement of the basis for your perceived need to do so.

Clinical Medicine vs. Insurance Underwriting

"There are major differences between the way a personal physician and an insurance company physician or underwriter view the same medical history."

Kathleen J. Greco, CLU
Guardian Life
BROKER WORLD
June, 1994, page 72

It is more than appropriate that this chapter includes a discussion of fundamental differences between clinical medicine, as practiced by your client's physician, and medical underwriting, as practiced by life underwriting professionals and their medical director consultants.

Clinical medicine is concerned with a person's present health status, maintaining good health and diagnosing and treating ailments.

Insurance underwriting is concerned with sorting risks into broad groupings. Those groupings are based upon mortality assumptions used by actuaries when pricing the insurance product. There may be just a few such groupings or, more typically, a dozen or even more. They go by such labels as "standard," "preferred," "table six," "table F," "decline," and so on.

Clinical physicians do not have, relatively speaking, the same time and expense restraints within which underwriters must work. They may see the patient many times before making their diagnosis, and as many times thereafter as they need to. Underwriters must act as expediently as possible; delays in issuing policies decreases the likelihood that those policies will be placed in force. Underwriters only "see" the proposed insured once per application. Thereafter, further encounters with that individual will be upon reconsideration of ratings or when new applications are submitted.

In terms of operating budgets, the differences between clinical medicine and insurance underwriting are so obvious that they do not need to be discussed. Within the constraints of the usual medical practice and the resources available from health insurance and the patient, clinical physicians do what they must to make a diagnosis and implement successful treatment. Underwriters have very limited budgets, most of which are allocated to routine screening that, in turn, is not subject to individual case discretion. Depending upon the impairment under scrutiny, the length of time the case has been pending, the amount of coverage applied for and, perhaps, other factors, the underwriter may be able to make limited use a very small range of additional tests on a *subset* of all his cases.

When clinical physicians challenge an underwriting decision, they might not be positioned to see that decision from the underwriter's perspective. The clinical physician's objections may be totally valid from a clinical perspective and, yet, still be out of focus with regard to what underwriting is all about. An example will help to clarify this matter.

As you read in Chapter 5, gamma-glutamytransferase (GGT) is a very prized component of the insurance screening blood profile. It is our most sensitive screening test for alcohol abuse. It is also highly sensitive to most kinds of liver and bile duct diseases.

In clinical medicine, GGT is often excluded from automated blood profiles. Even when it is included in a clinical profile, it is unlikely most physicians will react significantly to an isolated elevation.

The reason for this is inherent in GGT's perceived value as a diagnostic test. One major laboratory manual indicates that GGT has just one important use in diagnostic medicine; distinguishing between elevations of another enzyme test (alkaline phosphatase) that is due to liver impairments (GGT elevated) versus bone disorders (GGT normal). Suffice it to say, this is a rare scenario at best.

The sensitivity of GGT to most liver and bile duct impairments, to heavy drinking and the possibility of GGT elevation from medications, limits its perceived usefulness in the minds of clinical physicians who are attempting to make a diagnosis. Highly sensitive tests that are not very specific with regard to the reason they are elevated are not, generally, very helpful in clinical diagnosis.

Underwriters do not make a diagnosis—they want to establish insurability. For underwriters, it is sufficient to say that the GGT is elevated to such and such an extent and that, given a large group of people with that same degree of elevation, significant excess mortality would be expected *from the group*.

From all the findings in all of the studies that have been done in the four decades GGT has been used in medicine, there is no question that a group of 1,000 persons, all of whom have elevated GGT levels, will experience higher long-term mortality than an otherwise identical group of the same number of persons who have completely normal GGT readings. That forms the basis for the underwriter's decision to rate or decline an individual. At the same time, that perspective is utterly foreign to most clinical physicians and understandably so.

Communicating that point to clients and to their physicians is difficult. Still, in most cases, if the explanation is done in the manner described, it will be understood and accepted.

Remember, the insured's physician has the option of performing further tests. Medical reference books contain explicit protocols for the assessment of unexplained elevations of liver enzymes which occur in persons who do not appear to have a liver or related ailment. If such a workup is done, the underwriter will certainly agree to review the findings. In some cases, depending upon what further steps are taken by the physician (and what is discovered when those steps are taken), it might be possible to favorably improve the underwriting decision. Sometimes—not always.

The same logic used in the example regarding an elevated GGT test could be applied to any other medical impairment.

It all comes back to one basic consideration—fundamental differences in the focus of the clinical physician (good health, diagnosis) and the insurance underwriter (placing the insured in the appropriate large group of risks), so that the group yields a long-term mortality outcome within certain actuarial parameters).

CHAPTER 8

Emerging Technologies – What Agents Should Know

Every agent reading this book is aware of the changes that new technologies have brought to their daily work: premium quotes, illustrations, estate planning, policy administration and so on. All are processed electronically, whether by mainframe computer systems in home offices, local area network systems in agency offices, on laptop computers while you sit in a client's office, or even through internet web sites.

Electronic application completion and submission is a reality for many agents already. Such software prevents you from sending incomplete applications to the home office. It prompts you for company and regulatory requirements that must be submitted with the applications. Your personal productivity goes up; fewer cases are delayed by requests from underwriting departments for answers to incomplete questions or submission of missing forms; policies are issued more quickly; commissions are paid more promptly.

Expert Underwriting Systems

Expert underwriting systems began to make their appearance in the mid-1980s. For simple and uncomplicated applications that do not need additional requirements, approval could be accomplished in seconds! With the inclusion of a knowledge base, an expert system served as a decision support tool for underwriters. That is, the basic characteristics of a risk would be evaluated electronically and a recommended action would be made to the underwriter.

Whether an applicant had a history of a heart attack or skin cancer, the expert system could evaluate all the basic facts provided to it in seconds and present the underwriter with options for rating or further requirements. Actual decisions would remain the responsibility of a human underwriter.

Knowledge-based software allows an underwriter to have access to impairment and risk factor information with a few keystrokes. In the past an underwriter might consult an underwriting manual, a medical dictionary and a chief underwriter or medical director to gain a better understanding of an unusual or complex situation and the appropriate path to proper underwriting of the case. The expert system provides instantaneous access to such knowledge and resources and serves as a trainer and mentor simultaneously.

As medical and other risk factor information changes (new medical developments, changing mortality patterns, and so on), the knowledge-base can be updated at will. All the underwriters using an expert system can always be up-to-date on the latest trends wherever applicable and receive the most appropriate recommendations from the software. Consistency of decisions based upon similar facts is enhanced. Agents can feel confident that no matter which underwriter at a company sees their applications, random differences in underwriter interpretation of similar cases will be minimized.

Electronic Transmittal of Underwriting Requirements

Electronic transmittal of underwriting requirements by vendors such as laboratories, paramedical services, inspection companies and so on, is the primary delivery mode to home offices. Aside from the obvious time saved by eliminating mail and shipping of paper-formatted underwriting information, electronic transmittal allows expert systems to evaluate lab test results or paramedicals and approve uncomplicated cases immediately without human intervention.

Pen-based technology allows applications and examination forms to be completed with an "electronic pen" on a laptop computer and transmitted to a home office in lieu of paper submission (or in advance). At some future date, electronic signatures will be universally acceptable under states' laws. Many states are beginning to recognize electronic signatures as fully legal substitutes for the ink version.

Finally, imaging systems have been adopted by some companies to allow a paperless work environment. However, those systems are labor intensive for clerical personnel who must optically scan APSs, application forms and other documents into the computer system prior to actual service by the underwriting department. Machine-readable formats are being facilitated by electronic data interchange (EDI) improvements that minimize problems in data transmission between formerly non-compatible sites. It is likely that this format will supersede image processing in the future.

The Internet

Web sites for insurers and agencies are dramatically changing the way clients, agents and insurers interact. Information about products, rates and sales concepts is available to prospects on the Web that was never available in the past. Today's client might have already done his homework at several insurance companies and agencies web sites along with some investigation at insurance consumer information sites and state insurance department sites. More clients come to the table empowered with more knowledge and more intelligent questions than ever before.

E-commerce sites allow clients to actually get quotes and even apply and pay premiums on-line. Those web sites are "secured" using encryption technology so that private information cannot be "hacked" and seen by outsiders. In some cases, the interface with an insurer is through an agency web site, especially if state laws require a licensed agent to take an application.

Applying over the Internet is typically for modest amounts of coverage and for simple sales concepts such as personal programming, juvenile coverage and so forth. Sophisticated sales concepts requiring detailed needs analysis, coordination with other legal and financial advisors, establishment of trusts, etc., still demand face-to-face consultation or, at a minimum, telephone conversation. E-mail is likely to be inadequate for the extremely complex case.

Technological progress will continue unabated. Clients, agents and insurers are learning as they go with e-commerce. Everyone is developing new ways of thinking about how to sell insurance, how to provide service and how to underwrite. The empowered client is now on equal footing with agents and insurers. The knowledge gap has been narrowed.

CHAPTER 9

Inspection Reports and Other Investigative Information

Inspection reports are used by insurers to corroborate the information applicants give to agents and examiners. The reports also serve as a source of risk factor information that is secured by a disinterested third party (the inspection company) that insurers might not have asked about on their application forms (i.e., criminal arrest records). Every veteran underwriter has encountered situations where the applicant disclosed significant medical or nonmedical risk information to an inspector, but failed to properly answer the related question on the insurance application itself. From alcohol abuse to Zairean travel, applicants have had their reasons for not telling the insurer.

In-depth inspections, where multiple sources and references are directly interviewed, have fallen on hard times in recent years. A faster, less expensive alternative we have previously discussed—the personal history interview (PHI)—began to grow in popularity by the late 1970s and throughout the 1980s. Sometimes an insurer would establish a special unit of full or part-time home office employees to telephone applicants and conduct such interviews. Inspection companies began to combat their loss of revenue from street inspections by offering their own low-priced version of a telephone personal history interview, performed by their own personnel.

The use of personal history interviews is widespread today. It is likely to increase in the future because such interviews are fast, inexpensive and yield considerable protective value information pertinent to the risk being evalauted.

In this age of greater due diligence by insurers relative to the risks they assume, most still order traditional full inspection reports on very large cases. Regardless of the average size of your sales, you should have some knowledge of how PHIs and traditional inspections work and what you can do to minimize problems in this regard.

PHI callers and inspectors work from a questionnaire that might prompt them to additional, more detailed questionnaires, depending upon the prospect's specific answers to certain core questions. For example, "How much alcohol do you drink daily?" might be asked during the basic interview with the applicant. Depending upon the way that question is answered by the client, additional questions might be asked to amplify and clarify the details. The same is true for most medical impairments as well as risky occupations and avocations.

Working With an Inspection Company

Working with an inspection company requires mutual cooperation between the agent and the inspector/PHI caller. Helping arrange an appointment for the interview, obtaining correct names of references (i.e., attorneys, accountants, etc.), addresses, phone numbers and so on, will facilitate the efficiency and speed with which the report is completed and submitted to the underwriter.

The Fair Credit Reporting Act (FCRA) Pre-notice is not only mandated by law to be given to your client during the application process, but it also makes good business sense. A surprise phone call from the inspector to your client can be the killer of a sale. It is your job to make sure that your client has been given the notice, reads the notice and understands the notice. If the client does not understand the notice, you should be prepared to explain the purpose of inspections. You will need to illustrate how the reports help keep premiums low by minimizing insurer vulnerability to applicants who might choose to withhold risk information. Of utmost importance is your ability to explain how confidentiality of the inspection information is given the highest priority by both the inspection company and the insurer.

Consumer brochures are available from most inspection companies to give to your clients. They explain the purpose of inspections in plain language and will help your clients feel more comfortable when the interview call comes. Most inspection companies have one or more insurer clients review these brochures so the content is entirely acceptable and correctly stated.

Preparing Clients for Direct or Telephone Interviews

Preparing your clients for these essential interviews is the most important way you can minimize misunderstandings or unnecessary delays. First, you must eliminate the element of intrusive surprise and let the client know a stranger will ask personal questions. Now, you have removed the possibility that the client will refuse to be interviewed because he was not forewarned. Finally, you have done away with any resentment and the potential loss of the sale that might have come from your failure to warn the client that an inspection report would be performed.

Choosing references for inspectors to contact is especially critical to large amount inspection reporting. Attorneys, accountants, bankers and corporate treasurers generally have the best corroborative information pertaining to financial support for the death benefits requested. Those references should be authorized by your client in advance in order to share information with the inspector so that call backs between the inspector and reference source are unnecessary.

Public records such as state motor vehicle reports, bankruptcies and judgments, criminal records and so on are checked at the discretion of the insurer or as part of the comprehensive data search of various inspection products. It should not be surprising that underwriters often encounter information from these types of records that contradicts not only the application answers, but also the inspection interview answers given by the client. Discovering risk information in this fashion, even when it was clearly asked on the application, makes underwriters suspicious and apprehensive about the veracity of a client's candor. Naturally, an underwriter will wonder, "What else don't I know?" Even if the risk information discrepancy still leaves your client insurable, any equivocal situation will be decided in favor of the insurance company where lack of client candor has been discovered.

Motor Vehicle Records

Virtually all life and disability insurers ask about the prospective insured's driving record on the Part I. In addition, it is increasingly common for a copy of the insured's actual driving record to be designated as a routine requirement.

In the United States, state motor vehicle records (MVRs) are automated and, thus, can be obtained both easily and rapidly. They are comparatively inexpensive as well. Therefore, they are now perceived as a key source of underwriting information.

Historically, the use of MVRs was focused on young adult males. This was because that group was invariably associated with the highest rates of both alcohol/drug impaired driving arrests and overall motor vehicle mortality.

In recent years, with the increased emphasis on geriatric (over age 65) risks, underwriters have come to appreciate the value of the MVR in evaluating older age applicants. Motor vehicle reports are also often ordered electively for face amounts that are under the mandatory screening thresholds, if the insured is a private pilot or is engaged in any hazardous avocation. In addition, it is now more the rule than the exception that the underwriter will order a MVR if the applicant has unexplained liver enzyme elevations.

Trauma is a major cause of mortality and the leading cause of trauma death is motor vehicle accidents, and people who have adverse driving records are at an increased risk for fatal auto accidents. For all these reasons, MVRs are becoming more and more important as primary underwriting tools. We would not be surprised to one day soon see routine age/amount MVRs ordered at relatively low face amount thresholds, regardless of the admitted driving record, at ages 18 to 90 inclusive for both male and female insurance seekers.

Like motor vehicle authorities, underwriters utilize a point system for quantifying the significance of driving adversities. The highest points are assessed for driving while intoxicated (DWI) and driving under the influence (DUI). This is appropriate. Drunk and drugged driving are the most visible—and preventable—sources of excess motor vehicle-related mortality.

The growing use of MVRs in cases involving liver enzyme elevations reflects the close association between liver enzymes (especially GGT, which was explained in Chapter 5), alcohol abuse and the tendency to drive drunk. Several researchers have evaluated groups of drunk driving convicts to determine the prevalence of overt alcohol dependence. Their findings clearly show that DWI and DUI convictions are markers for alcohol abuse.

Study	% Drunk Drivers Meeting Criteria for Alcohol Abuse
Selzer (Michigan, 1977)	58%
Miller (New York, 1986)	73%
Redmon (Georgia, 1991)	90%

Post-notification forms are usually required by state or federal FCRA regulations whenever an adverse underwriting decision is based in whole or in part on inspection report details. Some FCRA regulations require that they be sent directly to the client, while others permit the agent to receive them for delivery to the client.

Typically, the client is instructed that the insurer's underwriting decision was influenced by information contained in the inspection report, and that a copy can be made available to the client. Any disputes over the accuracy of such information are between the client and the inspection company. A record of the client's dispute claim will be entered in the inspection company file and can be forwarded to the insurer, if so requested. The inspection company may be asked to reverify the original information and send a "corrected" report to the insurer.

If the insurer accepts the corrected information and it is deemed sufficient to change the underwriting action, a policy may be offered. However, the quality and veracity of the new information can only be judged by the insurer. If your client volunteers to freely discuss the nature of such information with you, you may be able to evaluate whether resubmission to the original insurer is worth pursuing.

The Medical Information Bureau

The Medical Information Bureau (MIB) might be the most misunderstood and miscast organization in the insurance world. Horror stories abound that portray the MIB as an Orwellian data bank where a "Big Brother" knows every aspect of people's lives. In actuality, life insurers organized the MIB as a non-profit association over 90 years ago for the purpose of minimizing their vulnerability to misrepresentation by applicants for insurance.

For example, if your client applied to ABC Life and told them he had three heart attacks in the past two years, he might be declined. If your client then applied to XYZ Life and chose not to disclose his cardiac history to them, how would XYZ Life protect itself? Through membership in the MIB.

Upon learning that your client had three heart attacks, ABC Life would have transmitted a series of numeric and alphabetic codes with identity information about your client to the MIB computers. These codes might (hypothetically) have read as follows: "911cde," where "911" represented "heart attack," "c" represented "information from attending physician," "d" represented "within two years," and "e" represented "three episodes." Such information is only accessible to insurance company employees (underwriters, medical directors, claims examiners, and so on) with a specific business need to know the information.

Upon receipt of your client's full, regular application to XYZ Life (or formal trial application) and the properly completed authorization form, that company would transmit his name, date of birth and geographic region to the MIB to search its records for a match. XYZ Life would receive the codes and initiate its own investigation by writing to health care providers named in the client's application. They would probably also ask you to re-question your client about his cardiac history "as we have reason to believe No. X on the medical questionnaire might not have been answered correctly."

In this matter of investigating the codes reported by the MIB, XYZ Life has no choice. By virtue of its membership, XYZ Life has agreed to abide by the constitution of the Medical Information Bureau which unequivocally prohibits member companies from making any underwriting decision based upon the MIB codes. To assure member compliance with MIB's rules and regulations, the MIB has an ongoing audit program. So if you ever hear someone claim a client was declined "because of his MIB record," do not believe it!

For disability income insurers, the Disability Income Record (DIR) protects insurers from exposure to overinsurance schemes. Applications to member companies for disability policies result in a report to the MIB of the monthly benefit amount and benefit period for which they have been applied. An applicant attempting to "stock up" on disability coverage by applying to multiple insurers and exceeding their individual issue and participation limits can be thwarted by use of the DIR. In this era of widespread excess disability claims experience by insurers, those protective mechanisms can save a company and its existing policyholders from many fraudulent claims.

You must deliver an MIB Pre-notice Form to every applicant which explains that a report of information obtained by the insurer may be made to the Medical Information Bureau. It advises clients that they have a right to know what information about them, if any, is contained in the MIB records, and that clients may pursue correction if any of the information is thought to be erroneous. The MIB's address is printed on the Pre-Notice Form. It is important that you correctly explain how the MIB protects policyholders of insurance companies from being victimized by new entrants into the insurance pool who have failed to disclose the risk information necessary for the insurer to charge the correct premium.

A consumer brochure, written in plain, understandable language, is available from the MIB that can explain to clients how the MIB works. *The Consumer's MIB Fact Sheet* is available by visiting their website www.mib.com (Consumer Information) or writing to:

Medical Information Bureau, Inc.
160 University Ave.
Westwood, MA 02090.

CHAPTER 10

Financial Underwriting: Does It Make Sense?

There is more likelihood of agent/underwriter conflict in financial underwriting than with any other subject. Time and again, after you have convinced your client of the need for the policy, the underwriters do not understand the rationale for the insurance plan or amount.

Where is the Loss?

Concepts of human life value are at the core of the life insurance business. Determining human life value to protect widows, children, other dependents and business partners is part of every sales agent's training. Tax planning concepts as a basis for using life insurance grew out of a legitimate desire to protect income and wealth. Yet, sales techniques that focused on "creating" wealth through life insurance often lead to misunderstandings between agents and underwriters with regard to the appropriate death benefit.

Wealth creation, if related to cash values, accumulation funds and dividends can be the primary motivation for the purchase of life insurance. However, wealth created solely by payment of a death benefit—that is, wealth which would not have been created by the insured during his natural life—is nothing more than speculation.

Despite recurring controversy over "needs analysis" as an appropriate sales method for life insurance, virtually all underwriters evaluate an applicant's needs in terms of potential economic loss from premature death. When evaluating the potential for "overinsurance," underwriters calculate:

- **Total death benefits in force with all insurers plus;**

- **The amount currently applied for with the underwriter's company plus;**

- **Concurrent applications to other insurers that will also be placed in force.**

Naturally, underwriters will take into account different purposes for different insurance policies when evaluating the total death benefits and various needs satisfied by policies in force and those for which applications have been made. Among these are:

- **family income replacement;**

- **estate taxes;**

- **debt cleanup;**

- **buy-sell;**

- **charitable giving;**

- **and others.**

Still, cumulatively the total coverage of insurance in all companies must make sense when compared to the applicant's potential earnings and wealth from a life uninterrupted by premature death. In sum, insurers cannot make applicants be worth more dead than they would have been worth alive.

Supporting Documentation

The most important supporting documentation you can supply is always a cover letter. Take nothing for granted when it comes to explaining the purpose of the insurance. Your skills, experience and professional education are different from those of the underwriter. The more unusual or sophisticated the insurance plan, the more important a cover letter becomes. Give the underwriter a complete financial picture of your client similar to that developed during your fact finding interviews. Describe how you arrived at the death benefit and illustrate any formulas used to calculate the necessary amount of coverage.

If you reviewed the client's tax returns, financial statements or other documents during your needs analysis, send copies to the underwriter along with your cover letter. Trust agreements, wills, buy-sell agreements and other special documents may be needed if the owner and beneficiary arrangements are unusual. Straight-forward arrangements for average amounts of coverage, such as basic family insurance on a working parent, probably will not require detailed documentation. However, you should anticipate extra scrutiny by underwriters for large amounts of insurance, third-party ownership or other unique situations.

Financial statements are required by underwriters to evaluate most large amount or "jumbo" insurance applications. You already know that analysis of financial statements is not an exact science because perfect accuracy is not the goal of most preparers. Estimates and data manipulation allow preparers to make financial documents say what they want them to say. For example, sales volume does not translate directly into profit and profit does not translate directly into spendable cash. Private companies may understate profits to minimize taxes while public companies may inflate profits to attract investors. Underwriters also know that what they see is not necessarily what they are getting. Your care in explaining and documenting such situations will minimize delays and adverse actions.

Basic accounting formats require balance sheets, income statements (or profit and loss statements), and cash flow statements (or statements of changes in financial position). Financial documents from successive years permit analysis of favorable or unfavorable trends, especially when ratio analysis is used. Underwriters know, like you, that a single year's financial data is a "snapshot" look at a person or business and does not necessarily paint a true picture of financial health.

Poor financial health can be an indicator of persistency risk, future personal or business bankruptcy, or a sign that your applicant is under severe emotional stress. Underwriters will be concerned about potentially serious business problems revealed by such key trends as:

- **recurring operating losses;**
- **working capital deficiencies;**
- **negative cash flows from operations; or**
- **adverse key financial ratios.**

Personal financial problems include a negative net worth, credit problems, charge-offs, judgments, bankruptcies and so on.

Personal or business asset valuation can be highly subjective. In business, intangible assets like patents, copyrights, trademarks, customer lists and goodwill that have perceived value to a specific business or industry must be carefully explained to underwriters. Any supporting evidence of a unique situation should accompany the financial documents. Overvaluation or undervaluation of assets is common for many reasons and you should explain those occurrences thoroughly.

Understatement of liabilities in business valuations may be done to attract buyers, investors or lenders. However, such deceit might leave a business vulnerable to charges of fraud and underwriters will not react favorably to such information. Fair market value formulas used in estate plans, buy-sell agreements, stock redemption agreements and so on, are subjective and highly variable. You should clearly illustrate those formulas used by your clients and provide supporting evidence for the underwriters.

Net profits might be artificially low (or shown as a loss) in a closely held corporation as part of a tax management strategy. You should explain this in advance to the underwriters and send supporting evidence of the true profit picture to alleviate concerns about the company's viability. If, in fact, a business keeps two sets of books to illegally avoid taxation, the underwriter will not be sympathetic. It is tough to swallow such explanations as "But the client wouldn't think of misrepresenting his financial picture to an insurer." Occasionally audited financial statements are deemed necessary by underwriters to provide a reasonable assurance of accuracy and an opportunity to review the opinions of the auditor.

Explaining Financial Underwriting

You often coordinate your needs analysis with a client's attorney, accountant, banker and other financial advisors. In a business insurance sale, you may work with a company's treasurer or comptroller. Since those people are serving your client also, they are obliged to guard the client's privacy. They might not be sophisticated about the varied uses of life insurance and challenge your recommendations. They might also resist the insurer's need for documentation from their files on the client. Nevertheless, you can control any misperceptions of intrusiveness when you ask for financial documentation and thereby minimize an all too common source of conflict among the underwriter, agent and client.

"Risk management" is a common topic with business people. Most financial professionals and advisors are assisting your clients in the proper management of their personal and business risks. You can use analogies between the underwriting process and risk management techniques to help your clients and their advisors understand the insurer's need for financial evaluation and supporting documentation.

Just as the investment banker must perform due diligence when a corporation is seeking to raise capital through the financial markets—just as the loan officer must diligently analyze credit risk—so must the insurance underwriter be duly diligent when evaluating the appropriate amount of insurance coverage. Financial underwriting requires thorough knowledge of the applicant's financial condition—earnings, investments, assets, liabilities and so on. Even though insurers do not pay out the face value until the time of a claim, their obligation begins immediately when the policy is placed in-force. For that reason, an insurer's $5 million death benefit risk is worth no less than a banker's $5 million loan risk.

One problem that is common in business insurance markets is that agents may be called by corporate risk managers and be treated as order-takers only. Low cost term insurance is usually the product of choice for business credit, key person and buy-sell situations, and many business clients have already decided what they need. They simply ask an agent to find companies that will write the coverage and to submit premium quotes. That kind of insurance shopping is common in property/casualty lines, but did not become prevalent in life insurance until the "term wars" of the 1980s.

In these situations, the agent has not done a needs analysis nor even seen the corporate financial statements. Some agents ask underwriters to talk directly with business clients or their advisors to explain the insurer's need for detailed financial documentation. Those agents would be better served if they were able to articulate the purpose of financial underwriting directly to clients and eliminate the risk of misunderstandings through a home office intermediary. Besides, not all insurers permit their underwriters to talk directly to clients of agents. For those that do, the agent should be satisfied that the underwriter is easily conversant in the language of business and financial analysis.

Insurable Interest and Insurable Value

Speculation, insurable interest, insurable value and violence potential all involve the public interest and public policy. The historical basis for an insurable interest is that speculation on human life through the purchase of insurance does not serve the public welfare because it can be an inducement to suicide or homicide. Public policy regarding insurable interest is founded on that principle which dates back to when speculators insured merchant ships before they set sail from English ports three centuries ago. The English Parliament in 1774 prohibited such speculation and established that insurers do, in fact, have an obligation to act in the public's welfare. Therefore, saving human lives by refusing to insure someone can be desirable public policy.

The vast majority of your applications will present no problem with regard to the need for an insurable interest between the owner and/or beneficiary and the proposed insured. Husbands, wives and children are the most common beneficiaries. The courts have long recognized the bonds of love and affection between married partners and children as evidence of a natural insurable interest. Concepts of insurable interest between unmarried domestic partners are evolving and, in some states, might be mandated. Business life insurance is also recognized by the courts as creating a proper insurable interest between owners, partners and key employees. In most situations, an obvious economic loss will be created by their premature death.

Insurable value refers to the amount of the economic loss, assuming insurable interest exists. Underwriters evaluate whether the total line of death benefits, in-force and applied for in all companies, is reasonably related to the prospective economic loss. To properly analyze insurable value, supporting documentation is necessary.

The violence potential is worrisome and difficult to evaluate. Red flags for underwriters include:

- **the absence of insurable interest;**
- **the presence of overinsurance; or**
- **any lack of candor about medical, financial or nonmedical risk information.**

The Society of Actuaries periodically conducts Large Amount Death Claim Studies. These reports have consistently shown that mortality is higher than expected on large amount policies in categories such as term insurance, creditor, buy-sell and key person. The most frequent causes of death are accidents, homicide and suicide. Talk with veteran claim examiners and you will hear numerous stories about scams, policy stacking and "accidental" deaths that occur before and after the contestable period.

"Yes, Virginia, there is a death benefit."

Universal life, interest-sensitive whole life, variable life, single premium life and assorted other non-traditional products often foster an interest in life insurance without regard to the death benefits. Among the serious problems created by this phenomenon is the generation of face amounts that have no relationship to the actual need. Low mortality charges and sales predicated on the future "return" for each premium dollar often make the life insurance benefit an afterthought in the sale. Through the use of aggressive illustrations, creative sales software and unique product designs, upper middle class and wealthy clients are often persuaded to put large sums of cash into such products thereby generating inordinately high face amounts.

Underwriters encounter many applications that "do not make sense" in the traditional way life insurance products are sold. To reduce agent and client misunderstandings, some insurers have created financial underwriting guides or brochures that establish "safe harbors" for agents selling creative products and concepts. Those companies' underwriting departments work with their sales departments to establish reasonable guidelines for maximum allowable coverages. If more companies encourage their sales and product professionals to sit down with their underwriters and agree ahead of time on financial underwriting limits, then agents will be the beneficiaries from knowing those tolerances before closing.

After all, why should you risk overselling a client at the point-of- sale only to have to later resell a smaller face amount or, worse, explain a declination for overinsurance? These episodes undermine your professional authority in a client's eyes. If an agent then sneers to a client about an insurer being too conservative (or angrily denounces an underwriting decision) the image of the agent, the company and the industry is hurt. Any trust and confidence earned during the sales interview might never be regained by the agent if he cannot deliver what was purchased.

Special Purpose Situations

Estate Conservation

For large amount applications, or unusual situations, you should provide the underwriter with a copy of your estate analysis and supporting documentation, such as your client's personal financial statement, preferably from a CPA. When a client's ownership interest in a closely held business represents a substantial portion of the estate value, the business financial statements should also be submitted.

Schedules of investments and copies of signed federal tax returns might be necessary for "jumbo" size applications or where some conflict arises. Certified appraisals of non-local real estate properties and investments, or art and other collectibles that represent a substantial portion of the estate value, are helpful for wealthy clients' applications. For coverage amounts in excess of that required by the estate analysis, you should provide a complete explanation and documentation.

Trusts

There are many different types of trusts, some of which can be very complicated. You should explain the purpose of the trust and disclose the ultimate recipients of the proceeds from all life insurance policies that fund the trust. After all, the basic principles of insurable interest and insurable value also apply to the ultimate beneficiaries of trust proceeds. Copies of a trust document may be necessary for large amount policies or unusual situations. When death benefits exceed the potential tax liability and/or asset loss to the trust beneficiaries, you should provide a logical explanation and documentation.

Charitable Giving

The traditional purpose of charitable giving life insurance is to protect against the loss of an applicant's contributions (cash, time or services). Tax deductibility of premiums and tax sheltering relative to estate plans are a vital part of the concept of using life insurance as a vehicle for charity. Underwriters establish charitable giving insurable interest by verifying a regular pattern of financial support or fund raising activities by the applicant.

You should provide a logical explanation to the underwriters when there is no previous pattern of giving or participation in the activities of a charity. Clear those situations for acceptability with the underwriters in advance. For unusually large amounts, provide certification of the contribution record from an official of the charity. Underwriters should be able to verify that schools, churches and other charities named as beneficiaries are legitimate and reputable organizations.

Juvenile and Older Age

Cash accumulation and investment products, especially single premium plans or "pour-in" riders, attract large premiums that can generate unusual face amounts. Life insurance products competing on rate of return emphasize the inside cash buildup rather than the death benefit. Underwriters must be satisfied that the owner and beneficiary designations not only satisfy the insurer's standards for insurable interest and value, but are in compliance with any applicable state laws regarding juvenile life insurance maximums. The net amount at risk may serve as the basis for death benefit evaluation in large, single premium policies.

The motivation to buy the policy and the potential for adverse selection are concerns when the premium payor or owner are not the parents or grandparents. Aunts, uncles and family friends are "third parties" and requests for ownership by them will require extra scrutiny by underwriters. Even if state laws allow such arrangements, the prudent underwriter will still expect a logical and easily corroborated explanation from the agent. In addition, the informed consent to the insurance purchase on a child's life should always be granted in writing by the parent(s).

Other unusual juvenile application situations will be carefully analyzed for risk of adverse selection. They include:

- **unequal coverage for siblings;**

- **death benefits that surpass those on a parent (even if state law permits);**

- **coverage on foster children, "prospective" adopted children and split-family children;**

- **absence of a pediatrician or family physician;**

- **reports of frequent or unexplained injuries or bruises in APSs or examinations;**

- **descriptions of musculoskeletal abnormalities, devices (such as leg braces, etc.), "slow learner" or "special child."**

With older age applicants, estate planning, tax sheltering and final expenses are common reasons life insurance is purchased. Elderly insurance situations that underwriters will carefully analyze for risk of adverse selection include:

- **adult children or third parties as owners and/or beneficiaries;**
- **absence of previous insurance in-force;**
- **a large death benefit without supporting income or net worth;**
- **economic dependence on adult children;**
- **adult child as premium payor;**
- **absence of a regular physician or health care provider;**
- **an entirely negative medical history;**
- **very recent medical problems;**
- **comments from an examiner or APS about slurred speech, walking aids, bruises, etc.**

Until recently, viatical companies used to purchase life insurance policies exclusively from terminally-ill policyholders to give them cash for expenses at the end of life. This was a creative way to help those with AIDS and other terminal illnesses make use of the death benefits for which they had paid premiums. However, in the latter part of the '90s, viatical companies began offering to purchase the policies of the elderly who were not terminally ill.

Insurers and regulators soon discovered that a few unscrupulous businesspeople were becoming involved in the viatical business. Regulators are now monitoring viatical companies more closely and establishing tighter regulations. In addition, the purchase of new polices by some elderly people was being made with the intent to immediately sell the policy to a viatical company for a cash portion of the death benefit. When the intent at the time of application is to resell the policy to a third party with no insurable interest, the insurer cannot allow the policy to be issued. Consequently, insurers and their underwriters are more closely monitoring the purchase of new life insurance policies by previously uninsured elderly applicants.

Key Person Insurance

The economic loss of a key person's skills, knowledge and business contacts because of premature death creates a legitimate insurable interest. Measuring the insurable value of a key person has traditionally been based on the amount of compensation paid multiplied by a factor representing the years needed to recover the loss and to replace the key person. Most insurers have used a multiplier between five and ten because a more objective formula has never been developed.

However, insurable value may also be based on:

- **the imputed value of patents held;**
- **specialized skills or knowledge;**
- **imputed lost corporate earnings; and/or**
- **corporate access to capital based upon the key person's long-term relationships with lenders and investors.**

These factors are subjective and difficult to quantify. Your thorough documentation and explanation of such calculations will contribute to an understanding of the death benefits requested. If there are other key persons in a company, they should also be insured to the extent of their insurable value.

For large amount or unusual cases, the most recent years' corporate financial statements and a signed employer verification of the key person's compensation, including regular bonuses, benefits and perks, are helpful. A copy of an employment contract showing all compensation details, including valuation of stock options, profit-sharing, etc., is appropriate when those are the applicable employment circumstances. Signed statements from those persons able to certify special key person values are also warranted, such as: corporate treasurer/CPA, patent attorney, commercial bank loan officer, investment banker, etc.

Buy-Sell / Stock Redemption / Cross Purchase / Survivorship Control

Underwriters rely on the value of the insured's ownership interest plus a modest growth factor to determine the appropriate face amount. Nevertheless, different businesses can have widely differing valuation formulas based upon their industry, geographic location and assorted other factors. Corporate net worth calculated in book value dollars usually differs significantly from market value. You should provide details of the formulas and supporting documentation used to determine the life insurance needed to fund the buy-sell agreement. Closely held corporate stock valuation is often a subjective exercise, but the formula is probably contained in the provisions of the stock redemption agreement.

Your cover letter should identify all business owners and their respective ownership percentage. Other owners or partners should also be insured under the agreement to the extent of their ownership interest. Corporate financial statements should be obtained and for large amount applications or unusual situations, a copy of the buy-sell agreement is appropriate. A draft copy or attorney's outline may be acceptable when the agreement and insurance applications are in process together. If any owner is uninsurable, a full explanation should be provided, including the means used to fund that owner's portion of the agreement.

Creditor / Business Loan

Lenders may require life insurance on a business owner(s) that assigns a portion of the proceeds to the lender to pay the outstanding principal balance due at the time of a premature death. Collateralized loans may be insured if the repossession of the collateral by the lender would place the business in jeopardy, but you should explain this to the underwriter. Not all insurers will cover collateralized loans. Insurable value is limited to the amount of the proposed insured's legal obligation as a guarantor for the outstanding principal balance at the time of the application.

All guarantors of the loan should be insured for the share of the loan proportionate to their ownership interest, and all substantial owners of the business should be guarantors of the loan. Otherwise, you should explain the reason any other eligible guarantors are not being insured or are being insured for unequal amounts. The policy should be owned by the business with an assignment to the lender "as their interest may appear."

You should provide evidence of the loan amount, purpose, terms and the names of the legal borrower and lender. For large amounts or unusual situations, submit a copy of the actual loan document and business financial statements (balance sheets and income statements). If insurance for more than 75 percent of the loan amount is required, you should explain why. If the lender is an individual (named or unnamed) rather than a reputable bank or commercial lender, full details and corroboration will be necessary. When substantial key person insurance exists, or when substantial personal insurance exists on the sole owner of a business, and it is not being assigned, explain the reasons to the underwriter.

A preliminary inquiry to the underwriter on large amount creditor insurance may be appropriate in most cases, anyway. If loan terms are less than five years, an early lapse may make the policy unprofitable and you may be encouraged to submit the application elsewhere.

Corporate-owned Life Insurance / Group Carve-out / Employee Benefit Life

There are a wide variety of employee benefit concepts using life insurance as the funding vehicle: Deferred Compensation, Split Dollar, Reverse Split Dollar, Group Carve-out and so on. You can help by providing the underwriters with cover letters and documentation verifying the underlying benefit plan, eligibility requirements and death benefit formulas used. Your special expertise in designing plans tailored to the individual needs of client employers might not be readily apparent from the application alone.

Insurable interest is usually satisfied by ownership/beneficiary designations that pay death benefits to spouses, families, or the estate of the insured, and that limit payments to the employer to the value of employer-paid premiums. Insurable value is typically evaluated within personal and estate conservation guidelines. For those policies that make a portion of the death benefit payable to the employer, key person guidelines may be applied by underwriters in the absence of other logical explanations.

If applications are perceived to involve eligibility violations, such as selecting only one executive for life insurance when a group of others in the same employee class should be eligible, they will be viewed unfavorably by the underwriters. Death benefits based upon unreasonable projections of length of employment and interest earnings may be perceived as arbitrarily maximizing the policy size.

Venture Capital and New Small Businesses

Until the early 1980s, few underwriters saw applications for business life insurance associated with a startup company. After all, most new businesses have other spending priorities during their formative years. But the phenomenon of venture capital investment created a desire to protect the investor's risk from the premature death of key persons involved in the startup enterprise. Investors felt their due diligence gave them an adequate picture of the business risks, but key person mortality risk was beyond their ability to evaluate.

Venture capital applications typically involve:

1. **Private placements through:**

   - **wealthy private investors;**

   - **institutional investors (pension funds, insurers, etc.);**

   - **small business investment companies (often subsidiaries of banks or other companies);**

   - **investment clubs or pools of private investors.**

2. **Loans from commercial or private sources:**

   - **Small Business Administration guaranteed bank loans.**

Historically, more than half of all new businesses fail within five years of their startup. That poses significant risks for poor persistency compared to mature companies. For that reason alone, insurers are uncomfortable with venture capital and new, small business life insurance requests. Insurable interest in those applications is similar to key person or creditor insurance. Insurable value is estimated prospectively when the key person is the purpose, and by loan value when creditor insurance is the purpose.

You should contact the underwriters in advance to see if they will even consider insurance coverage for a new venture. If so, submit copies of any venture capital agreement or loan documents that illustrate the amount advanced and name the parties to the agreements. A copy of the business plan is essential to underwriters and the critical portions will include the market analysis and pro forma financial statements. Underwriters must know whether the investment or loan is for a startup company (1-3 years), later-stage company (4-6 years) or is follow-on capital (7 years or more). The policy ownership should be by the new company with the lender or investor named beneficiary "as their interest may appear."

Key person formulas might be exotic for some new ventures and most insurers will not cover all of the potential loss. If projected profitability is expected within three years, and all other aspects of the business and health risk are favorable, 50 percent or less of the potential loss is likely to be the most that the underwriters will consider. High risk ventures in biotechnology or similar fields might not project profitability for seven to ten years. For that reason, even less life insurance coverage may be available. The best approach for you and your client is to request a preliminary review by the underwriters prior to submitting a formal application.

A developing problem with e-commerce businesses has underwriters reacting very cautiously. Many of the recent IPOs of internet-based businesses (business-name.com) have been outrageously overvalued. In the Wild West atmosphere of the Internet, many investors are wagering huge sums of money on the e-commerce revolution. Yet, they are not performing adequate due diligence. Many e-commerce businesses will fail after the owners have taken the investors' money and run. Life underwriters *will* use due diligence; agents should, too.

Additional Reading

1. Will, Charles A., *Life Company Underwriting*, 1974.

2. "Venture Capital and Funding New Ventures," John Krinik, *ON THE RISK*, Vol. 4, No. 1, December, 1987.

3. "Funding New Ventures: Risk Appraisal Considerations," John Krinik, *ON THE RISK*, Vol. 4, No. 2, March, 1988.

4. "Point of View: Overinsurance Kills," Charles A. Will, *ON THE RISK*, Vol. 4, No. 4, September, 1988.

5. "Where's the Loss? The Financial Underwriting Flashpoint," John Krinik, *PROBE*, June 24, 1991.

6. "Financial Underwriting of New Small Businesses," John Krinik, *ON THE RISK*, Vol. 9, No. 2, March, 1993.

7. "Insurable Interest: California Speculates on the Value of Human Life," John Krinik, *PROBE*, June 6, 1994.

8. "Safe Harbor or Fallacy?: The Agent/Home Office Partnership," John Krinik, *PROBE*, November 21, 1994.

CHAPTER 11

Nonmedical Risks – Aviation, Avocations and Occupations

The risks people take for recreation or for their work sometimes jeopardizes their health, and occasionally their life. "Extreme sports" have become part of the popular culture thanks to television coverage. "Pushing the envelop" or "taking it to the limit" are institutionalized concepts within the competitive nature of business and society in the 21st century.

Aviation and Avocations

Reports of mountain climbing deaths occasionally make the daily news. And certainly the highest peaks offer more than enough danger to experienced climbers, let alone to weekend enthusiasts. Yet, more pervasive is the growing culture of risk-takers whose anthem sounds like a soda pop commercial—"Been there. Done that." Sky surfing, cliff parachuting, heli-skiing and so on are but the latest examples of exciting and dangerous sports where victory is measured by staying alive.

Such sports as "extreme skiing" may involve flying a helicopter to a previously unskied mountain in New Zealand and risking avalanches, helicopter crashes or mountain falls. The promoters of such adventure experiences solicit customers who are fit, aggressive, experienced and proficient. They may be standard medically, but a flat extra premium will probably be needed to cover that risk...if the insurer is comfortable assuming the risk.

It is not unusual for a private pilot to fly his plane to a vacation spot for a weekend of scuba diving. Such "jet set" relaxation can leave the person brain dead or just plain dead if the pilot has not allowed enough time before diving into the depths.

Not just those in the twenty to thirty-something age range pursue these exhilarating and death-defying sports lifestyles. The youthful culture of successful babyboomers now in their forties and hitting age fifty encourages many two-day per week athletes to push their bodies as hard as they did twenty years earlier. Broken limbs, torn ligaments, fractured skulls and other musculo-skeletal injuries can leave the victim with residual problems of a chronic and sometimes debilitating nature. Disability income exclusions have to be expected unless waiting periods are sufficiently long (90 days and up) and the occupation duties are essentially sedentary.

Even your gray market clients may be using their golden years to see the world and experience adventures that time and circumstance did not permit them during their working years. Geriatric doctors now see patients who go trekking in the Himalayas, sometimes despite serious medical problems. Diabetes, heart disease, respiratory ailments, arthritis, and so on are not necessarily immobilizing to today's senior citizen. But underwriters must recognize and evaluate these risks.

Whether your application for such a client is processed quickly and favorably depends a great deal upon the degree of detail you provide. Most companies have an aviation supplement form that often has been approved by state insurance departments for inclusion in the policy itself. However, the use of avocation or occupation supplement forms is inconsistent between various insurers.

Quite simply, the fundamental factors that an underwriter will evaluate when the risk involves aviation, avocation or occupation are:

- **The specific nature of the activity. Skydiving, auto racing and skin diving are general terms for activities within which the degree of risk can vary substantially. A recreational skydiver has a different risk than a professional stunt skydiver; a weekend rally auto racer has a different risk than a professional Indy style racer; a shallow water skin diver has a different risk than a deep water scuba diver.**

- **The past and expected frequency of the activity as measured by both how often the activity is performed and the number** of times it is done at varying degrees of risk. A skin diver who consistently dives to no more than 30 feet, three or four times per year, presents a different risk than a diver who plumbs depths of 100 feet or deeper six or more times per year. A private pilot who flies 75 hours per year presents a different risk than one who flies 300 hours per year.

- **The past and expected locations of the activity.** Flying in the wilds of Alaska or around mountainous terrain presents different risks than flying from Atlanta to Tampa; skin diving off the coral shores of a Carribean island presents a different risk than professional deep sea diving in the seas of the Indian Ocean.

- **The past and expected conditions of the activity.** Flying at night and under adverse conditions to meet deadlines for pay presents a different risk than flying only under favorable conditions recreationally; racing mini cars on tracks with speed governors presents a different risk than professional NASCAR racing.

- **The limits of the activity.** How high? How deep? How long (duration or distance or both)? How far? How fast? How often at these limits? These factors provide objective criteria to help the underwriter price the risk.

- **The experience of the applicant.** A beginner? Always accompanied by a "buddy" or co-pilot? Always under organized supervision or association? A veteran? An instructor of others?

- **The certifications, if any, of the applicant.** Does the sport or activity have a training program (or sanctioning body) leading to a certificate of proficiency? If so, has the applicant obtained it? If there is a graded program of proficiency, what levels have been achieved to date? If a copy of the official certificate is available, send a copy.

- **The amateur or professional status of the applicant.** Does the applicant ever participate for money or cash-equivalent awards? The risks associated with pure recreational activity are different than the risks associated with activities involving financial gain; they might be lesser or greater depending upon the circumstances.

Take a look at this chart:

Avocations — Extreme Sports

Activity	Fatalities per 100,000 participants
Power Boat Racing	71
Mountaineering	50
Homebuilt Aircraft	312
Balloon	67
Skydiving	25
Sources: U.S. Hang Gliding Association; National Safety Council; Diver's Alert Network	

One of the highest accident mortality rates is associated with powerboat racing—71 fatalities per 100,000 participants. Compare that to skydiving fatalities at 25 per 100,000 participants, hang gliding at 40 deaths per 100,000, and scuba diving at 47 fatalities per 100,000. Among the questions you should provide answers to for a powerboat racer are:

- type of racing: closed course, drag, marathon, offshore, straightaway, time speed trials or otherwise;

- type of craft: (hydro, runabout, etc.);

- class of competition;

- professional or amateur;

- number of races in the past twelve months;

- number of races in the next twelve months;

- average length (miles, laps, etc.);

- average speed and top speed;

- any changes anticipated in the next twelve months (class, boat, etc.);

- any citations, fines, sanctions, etc.

Your comprehensive report submitted with the application to the underwriter will serve to expedite the most favorable decision possible. Do not let the underwriter discover from an inspection report that your client has been fined, cited, suspended, or otherwise been considered irresponsible in his activities. Give the underwriter the complete details up front. A technical violation might be viewed favorably compared to a flagrant violation; it will be a judgment call.

Although commercial aviation is often quoted as being safer than driving a car every day, private aviation is a different story. Remember the death rates previously mentioned for sports activities? The fatality rate for general (private) aviation is 145 per 100,000 participants. For homebuilt aircraft it runs 312 per 100,000 and for air show flying it is 500 fatalities per 100,000!

Insurers have seen their aviation mortality climb over the past two decades. This has been especially acute in the large case blocks of business. Of course, this would make sense because people who can afford to own or fly a plane typically have enough money to purchase larger death benefit policies. Of interest to insurers has been the frequency with which alcohol played a role in the aviation mortality and the patterns that have emerged of reckless or drunken driving incidents in the deceased aviators' lives. It would be wise to prepare such clients for possible adverse decisions when you become aware of such histories during the sales process.

Occupations

As a result of intense job safety efforts by governmental bodies such as the Occupational Safety and Health Administration (OSHA) and the business community, on the job mortality has improved significantly since World War II. Occupational underwriting was once one of the critical risks evaluated by underwriters. With the increasingly sedentary nature of jobs and occupations in the dawning information age, current exposure by applicants to acute hazards is less significant than in the past for the general population.

However, occupational medicine and toxicology have become important fields of study and specialized treatment, and many white collar and professional workers—chemists, laboratory technicians, etc.—are regularly exposed to chemical or pathological toxins. These people are usually well-paid and make attractive prospects for individual ordinary life and disability insurance. So your sensitivity to the occupational hazard information will be critical to your sales success.

Genetics research has revealed that a single toxic molecule can damage DNA. Constant assault by toxins through the respiratory system or the skin can overwhelm cellular defenses and initiate malignant cell activity. Anyone constantly exposed to fumes, dusts or other inhaled irritants is vulnerable to developing respiratory disease (emphysema, chronic obstructive lung disease, etc.). Some toxins might affect neurological physiology in insidious ways over time or be a catalyst for malignancy.

Geriatricians have begun paying special attention to occupational histories of the elderly patients. Your elderly clients who have accumulated wealth and need life insurance protection might have spent the past forty years occupationally exposed to toxins. Only now might they have begun to exhibit serious symptoms. You can prepare the underwriter for such findings in advance by explaining what you know about your elderly client's lifelong work and exposures in the cover letter. The underwriter will be able to use this background information, that typically would not have been known or understood, to make a more informed and fair decision for your client.

CHAPTER 12

Disability Products

Differences From Life Underwriting

Disability income is a casualty product. It can be used to pay multiple claims of varying durations while it remains in-force. For that reason alone, it must be underwritten differently than life insurance. After all, for life insurance there is usually one primary and potential claim payment—upon the death of the insured. That is, the insured must die to collect. On the other hand, disability insurance is a living benefit. Life insurance options like disability waiver of premium, accidental death benefit and accelerated death benefits notwithstanding, there are simply more opportunities for disability insurance policyholders to manipulate the product to their advantage.

Consequently, two key factors—*stability* and *motivation*—are evaluated by underwriters along with the obvious sickness and accident hazards. Stability of income and occupation have traditionally been viewed as predictors of favorable claims experience. Yet with the massive changes taking place in the global economy, and the effects of technology on people's job stability, motivation is taking over as the most reliable risk factor of the two.

Evaluating motivation requires knowledge of the applicant's education and training, professional or job track record and degree of lost earnings as a result of disability. These risk factors help underwriters judge the potential for malingering in the event of a disability. The increasing emphasis on motivation in disability underwriting can actually work to your advantage when submitting applications to the underwriter. Why? Because it gives you an opportunity to paint a more thorough picture of the applicant for the underwriter than could ever be gleaned from just the application forms.

Using the cover letter, you can give the underwriter a virtual resume or curriculum vitae of your client: education and training, job and professional history, business successes and so on. You can help the underwriter better understand why your client would be highly unlikely to malinger in the event of a disability, why your client cannot afford to be away from his job or business for any extended period of time and why your client would not be inclined to do so anyway.

Exclusion Riders, Ratings, Modifications

There are more occasions when adverse action is taken in disability underwirting than in life underwriting. In fact, nearly 40 per cent of disability applications have historically been modified at issue and at least 10 per cent have been declined. By comparison, life applications are issued as applied for at least 90 per cent of the time.

The most common disability modification is the exclusion rider—with or without a substandard premium. Most exclusion riders are used when the disease or disorder can be narrowly defined as to anatomic location, organ system or self-limiting manifestation.

The most common exclusion rider is for back problems—"any injury to or disorder of the spine, its muscles, ligaments, discs, or nerve roots"— or wording similar to that. Musculoskeletal disorders are among the most frequent causes of disability, but they cannot always be objectively evaluated during a claim. Unless someone has a visible injury such as a fracture, the degree of impairment and inability to perform the duties of one's occupation can be nearly impossible to objectively quantify. In addition, there is a high degree of association between mental and nervous stress and both the incidence and severity of back problems.

Ratings are typically used when there is an increasing risk and/or multiple organ system risk, such as with high blood pressure, elevated cholesterol, abnormal glucose, and so on. Ratings can range from 10 per cent to 200 per cent extra, but it is uncommon to see ratings applied at either extreme. The larger the rating, the shorter the allowable benefit period. For example, a 25 per cent extra might permit the issue of a "To Age 65" benefit period, but a 50 per cent rating might require a maximum "5 Year" benefit. When a rating reaches 75 per cent or higher, it is common to cap the benefit periods at 2 or 1 years, assuming the insurer even offers those products.

In recent years, occupation class and benefit amount modifications based on issue and participation limits have probably become the most common nonmedical modifications. Adverse claim experience throughout the 1980s and into the 1990s provoked many insurers to drop disability insurance from their portfolio. The leading reinsurers of disability for three decades left the market in the '90s. Those insurers remaining in the DI market became quite conservative in their evaluations of occupational duties and adequate income. Management or professional class duties involving any exposure to physical labor or hazards are treated with greater caution than in years past.

For these reasons, the cover letter detailing an applicant's duties will be critical to obtaining the most favorable occupation class possible. Any physical or manual labor or exposure to sickness or accident hazard should be explained thoroughly, with breakdowns of the numbers of hours daily or weekly that your client spends on those duties. In the case of business owners requesting the higher occupation classes, you should provide the percentage of time spent on physical or hazardous duties compared to executive, management and supervisory duties.

You know the client—you have talked to the client—and you might have visited his place of business. Nobody is in a better position to explain what your client does than you. Here is a typical breakdown:

- **Executive duties (strategic planning, product development, marketing promotion, etc.): 5 to 8 hours daily—64 per cent and up;**

- **Supervisory and training on shop floor: 1 to 2 hours daily— 12 per cent, approximately;**

- **Direct machine operation: 1 to 2 hours daily—12 per cent, approximately;**

- **Payroll, accounting, personnel: 1 to 2 hours daily—12 per cent, approximately.**

Total hours daily: up to 16, as necessary.

That kind of detail can mean the difference when you are attempting to obtain the most favorable occupation class that might be available. It can also minimize misunderstandings in the event the client actually does have to file a claim at some future date.

Psychiatric Impairments and Disability Insurance Underwriting

Psychiatric impairments are common. At least 15 per cent of American adults, if tested, would meet established diagnostic criteria for a psychiatric disorder.

Psychiatric impairments are chronic, recurring illnesses that often last a lifetime. Since they directly affect the highest capacities of humans, it should come as no surprise that in one study of over 25,000 subjects, depression had a stronger link to physical disability than the severity of any coexisting physical diseases.

Psychiatric impairments are the leading cause of long-term disability claims. This has obvious implications for producers submitting DI applications.

The underwriting of individuals with a history of any type of psychiatric impairment must be conservative. After all, when a disability claim is filed for a mental or nervous disorder, evaluation of the symptoms is a subjective process. Unlike a broken leg that can be clearly seen and objectively assessed as it heals, evaluation of mild to moderate psychiatric symptoms usually depends upon the patient's description of them to his physician. If a claimant is prone to malinger in order to avoid losing his monthly disability check, the insurer may be vulnerable to such manipulation.

There are several things the producer can do to get the most favorable consideration for his client in the face of an acknowledged (or implied) psychiatric history:

- **The Golden Rule: The more information, the better! Make sure a *detailed* medical history is recorded, either by yourself (non-medical) or by the examiner. Succinct, one sentence histories ("Depression, three years ago, no problem now.") are too ambiguous. That leads to conservative decisions.**

- **Avoid vague terminology like "nervous breakdown." Identify the impairment as diagnosed by your client's caregiver. Remember, within any broad category of psychiatric impairments, such as anxiety disorders or affective (mood) disorders, there are *both less favorable and more favorable* risks.**

- **Focus on the impact that the impairment has had on your client's work history:**

a. The number of "sick days" attributable to this condition; and

b. The impact on his ability to perform his job duties.

- Physicians may use certain non-specific or ill-defined labels to describe what amounts to, in reality, depression. When an "impairment" such as fatigue or insomnia is recorded on the Part II, it will appropriately arouse the underwriter's suspicions. Amplify the history; provide as many details as possible.

- Some "psychiatric" consultations are related to marital difficulties. Such problems might or might not lead to disability. Once again, it is essential to provide the underwriter with as many details as possible. It is to be hoped that the practitioner who has seen your client for this history will do likewise. Reports from psychiatric caregivers (and from primary care physicians when writing about a psychiatric history) tend to be too brief, omitting details that might allow more favorable underwriting assessment.

- Certain psychiatric medications, most notably the so-called selective serotonin reuptake inhibitors, which includes Prozac (fluoxetine), Zoloft (sertraline), Paxil (paroxetine), and Celexa (citaloprim), and the benzodiazepine drug Xanax (alprazolam), are widely prescribed for both psychiatric impairments and for other disorders. The underwriter will correctly presume that anyone taking Prozac, Zoloft, Paxil, or Celexa is suffering from depression. If, in fact, a very different diagnosis has been made, it is essential that this exact diagnosis be spelled out in as much detail as possible by the insured (Part II, signed statement) and physician/caregiver (APS).

- Maximize the underwriter's flexibility by applying for the longest disability insurance waiting period your client can accept. Some impairments will trigger adverse decisions on applications seeking 30-day or 60-day waiting periods but can be underwritten more favorably at 181 days or longer.

How Elimination Periods, Benefit Periods and Other Options Offer Solutions to Disability Problems

If you are selling disability to a client with a known impairment, you have a much better chance of receiving a standard, unmodified policy if you ask for a long waiting period. Disability underwriting manuals illustrate lower ratings and/or fewer exclusions for impairments when applications request elimination periods of 90 or 180 days. For example, if your client had an isolated back problem that did not last long, and with recovery some time previous to the date of the application, the underwriting guidelines might not require an exclusion if the elimination period is 90 days or longer. Yet the same application with a 30-day waiting period would have a far greater probability of being issued with an exclusion rider.

Elimination periods in disability insurance are analogous to the deductible amounts in medical expense, auto or fire insurance. Most clients today are so sensitized to the use of deductibles as a means to save premium dollars that they should be receptive to suggestions to purchase longer elimination periods.

In addition, if your client is applying for a long-term benefit period, the need for an exclusion or rating would also increase. For example, a history of high blood pressure, with only moderate control (where the primary risk is for the development of heart disease), would be viewed far less favorably if long-term benefits were requested than if "5 or 2 Year" benefit periods were requested. After all, with average life expectancy increasing, even for impaired risks, a lifetime benefit could extend claim payout for decades.

Other potential options to consider decreasing or deleting (depending upon the policy configurations offered by the insurer) include: "own occupation" riders and future purchase option riders—riders that create potential, additional risk.

Financial Underwriting: Income, Buy-out, Key Person, Overhead Expense

The bottom line with disability financial underwriting is to answer the question, *How much income will be lost in the event of the proposed insured's disability under the terms of the contract?*

To assist the underwriter with income evaluation, thoroughly clarify the income included in your needs analysis. This may include more than just salary. Income, especially for the self-employed or for owners of small businesses, may include retained earnings of the business. That is a common maneuver to help fund growth and/or minimize personal taxation of the owner. In addition, employee benefits provided to the owner such as health insurance, pension contributions, and so on, are often lost when the business owner is disabled and cannot personally generate business income. Company cars that double as personal vehicles are another "perk" with income value that may be lost during an extended period of disability. The underwriter may be able to include some or all of such imputed income towards determining the issue limit subject to the insurer's rules and practices. However, it is critical to explain it all in a cover letter supplemented by the appropriate documentation (tax records, income and expense statements, etc.).

Unearned income, if significant, may be used as a debit against the total amount of earned income counted towards the issue and participation limits. The logic of doing this is associated with the probability that unearned income—investment income, pension income, etc.—typically continues to be received without regard to whether the client works or not. However, the business owner who takes a lower salary in favor of reinvesting the company revenues in the business, or leaves the revenues as retained earnings, may actually suffer a loss of such income if he becomes disabled and cannot manage his business. You must clearly explain to the underwriter *how loss of business income will happen if the client cannot work* and *how much income after expenses would actually be lost.* Beyond that, and depending upon the company's published guidelines for submitting proof of earnings, you should gather all the supporting evidence of earnings that will support your client's contention that his "unearned" income would be lost in the event of his disability.

When submitting financial documents, especially tax returns, more companies are requiring two or three years of returns rather than only the current year's return. That is because incomes today are unstable and if the most recent year for which the applicant is quoting his income is an aberration, the prudent and equitable income figure for the underwriter to use would be an average of the past several years' earnings.

Undocumented income is far less likely to be counted today towards higher issue limits. If a client claims to be earning any substantial "cash" income, unreported to the tax authorities, the underwriter should not count it towards the income and participation limits. No doubt the client will tell you that he is "only cheating the IRS" and would never think of cheating the insurer...

Yeah, right.

Do not be gullible and do not expect your underwriter to be taken in either.

Specialty products like Key Person Disability and Disability Buy-Out have much in common with their life insurance counterparts. You must clearly explain how the proposed key person's disability will result in a financial loss to the employer or business, and then you must illustrate how you quantified it. Supporting documentation (sales revenues for which the applicant is directly responsible, etc.) that ties directly to the quantifiable loss should accompany the application.

Disability Buy-Out requires business valuation evidence, and some insurers require a copy of the buy-out agreement within the first policy year. Despite the usual one or two-year elimination period on this product, the benefit amounts are usually substantial and often paid in a lump sum under "presumptive disability" clauses. For these reasons, the same due diligence exercised on a life buy-out must be applied to disability.

Overhead Expense coverage is typically reimbursable dollar for dollar for specific covered expenses up to a maximum benefit amount set by the insurer that must be itemized and, in the event of a claim, receipted. Some expenses, like depreciation, are viewed differently by different insurers. Discuss these topics with your insurer and know what it is prepared to cover and what documentation it requires.

Income replacement coverage is the replacement product for traditional occupational disability products. The policy language does not even refer to "disability" and is predicated on loss of earnings as a result of sickness or accident rather than the inability to perform occupational duties. The income loss documentation for these products is, of necessity, more stringent than for occupational disability coverages.

CHAPTER 13

Special Products and Markets

Immigrants

The fastest growing demographic market in the United States and Canada for the past twenty years has been that of immigrants. Most have come to North America from the developing nations of the world where employment opportunities have traditionally been limited. In addition, laws passed in the early 1980s liberalized restrictions on immigration for two reasons:

1. To attract foreign investment capital—that is, wealthy immigrants who could demonstrate their plans to start businesses in North America and create new jobs would be given certain preferences.

2. To attract a larger labor force that would enlarge the tax base in the early 21st century as huge numbers of baby boomers retired, thereby straining the Social Security and Medicare/Medicaid systems.

Of course, unforeseen economic and political changes have altered the dynamics of what lawmakers anticipated fifteen years ago. Nonetheless, immigrants represent a large and growing market for insurers to serve.

Language / Ethnic Marketing

Many companies that market their products and services to immigrants and other ethnic groups realize that many of those consumers do not speak or read English fluently, if at all. Although second generations are usually bilingual, with English as the primary spoken language, the first generation immigrant might never learn enough English to read an insurance policy and understand it.

For that reason, some insurers who target the ethnic markets print their sales literature and policy forms in languages other than English. In fact, some states have taken notice of the potential vulnerability of non-English speaking insurance buyers and either have, or are considering, requiring insurers to take steps to assure that insurance buyers understand the contracts into which they are entering. Even in states without such legislation, potential litigation exposure is a sufficient liability risk to provoke insurers to be certain that translation of application forms and policy language is made available prior to closing a sale.

Even insurance vendors, such as paramedical firms and inspection companies, hire multilingual employees so that questions asked during an examination or inspection can be understood by the proposed insureds. This is the bottom line for all insurance agents in a multicultural marketplace: be certain that any prospective client you are working with who does not have full verbal and written command of English has access to the translation of your sales and contract materials in their spoken language. A relative or trusted friend of the applicant can often fill that role.

Financial and Cultural Nonmedical Issues

The privacy of personal and business financial information is an important concern of North Americans. In other cultures it is also important, sometimes to the extent that it is almost impossible to obtain copies of financial statements or documentation. If they even exist, they might exist in several variations—analogous to a business that keeps a different set of books for different purposes.

When you conduct your fact finding and needs analysis, it is incumbent upon you to be able to convincingly explain to the underwriter why financial documentation is unavailable. If an insurer declines to participate, be prepared to work with a different insurer on the case. However, do not do so until you have at least provided some evidence of your client's assets and liabilities, even if it is not in the form of formal financial statements. Signed letters from the client's bank officer, attorney, accountant or some other third-party with professional qualifications may be adequate for some insurers depending upon the amount at risk. If the client is working or operating a business in the U.S. or Canada, there must be tax records that can help establish the client's net worth and income.

Hepatitis / Regional Diseases

Hepatitis B is endemic to many parts of Asia. Asian immigrants often became infected during childhood, but the long latency period might result in delayed symptoms of liver disease until the third or fourth decade of life, if not later. Be prepared for frequent findings of abnormal liver results on the blood tests of your Asian immigrant clients. The risk of cirrhosis and eventual liver cancer is quite high in those populations.

Immigrants from the tropical regions of the world can be exposed to other infectious diseases—cholera, malaria, and so on. They cannot all be evaluated within the context of available underwriting tests. Yet, travel to those regions of the world where such diseases are endemic may require flat, extra premiums to cover the risk of exposure to such diseases or the lack of adequate health care.

To illustrate the potential problem for insurers, one reinsurer recently related the following story:

> A wealthy Mexican business executive, who spent considerable time traveling to and residing in the United States, applied for a $10 million life insurance policy. All the medical and nonmedical evidence was entirely favorable and the policy was approved as applied for. Within one year after the policy was issued, the insured made a return trip to his rural Mexican village for a family celebration. Sanitation facilities were not up to modern standards and some of the local dishes prepared for the feast included foods that were washed in the local water supply and served uncooked. Within 48 hours of eating that food, the business executive exhibited symptoms of cholera and died.

The lesson for the insurer and reinsurer was to be sure the premiums for risks that cannot be screened during underwriting are built into the products sold to non-domestic populations.

International Residents

Legal Issues

You have probably submitted an application on a client who is a citizen of another country, whether he is a recent immigrant or actually lives and works outside the U.S. The global economy fosters the growth of more multinational corporations and international partnerships. Most insurers will require proof of intent to establish permanent residency via a "green card" if the applicant is an immigrant. The immigrant who is only in the U.S. temporarily presents a risk unacceptable to many domestic insurers because of the difficulty of performing claims investigations in areas of the world where it does not do business already nor have any local contacts.

Taking an application on U.S. soil for a foreign national may be legally acceptable under state insurance laws. However, should a contestable death claim be filed outside the U.S., that country's laws will probably take precedence. It is always wise to obtain clearance in advance from insurers before taking an application on a foreign citizen who resides outside the U.S. Clarify the legal issues before committing the insurer to the terms of the contract.

Financial Underwriting

For those companies that conduct international business, they establish protocols for underwriting "foreign nationals" outside the United States. Typically, they may insist on evidence of asset ownership in the U.S. or employment by a multinational U.S. corporation.

As mentioned previously with regard to immigrants, foreign nationals may be extremely reluctant to share financial evidence with you or the insurer. The kind of due diligence performed by U.S. and Canadian underwriters with respect to financial evaluation is uncommon elsewhere in the world. There tends to be more reliance on the personal knowledge of agents, brokers and bankers, and more credence given to the ability to simply pay the premiums.

It is important to understand that life insurance products outside the U.S. have traditionally been more analogous to endowments, having more emphasis on the savings element. With proportionately smaller death benefits, more rapidly decreasing net amounts at risk, and higher premium levels, the risk of overinsurance is significantly reduced. Premium affordability is a justifiable basis for evaluating the financial status of applicants.

That approach is changing as products in Europe and Asia become more competitive and premiums fall, thereby allowing larger death benefit purchases and more risk of adverse financial selection. There is growing interest in the North American approach to financial underwriting.

For the time being, when you are working with a foreign national client, utilize whatever resources for financial information might be available. If the client works for an American company, request a formal letter from the employer verifying salary and other forms of remuneration. Request a signed verification from U.S. banks regarding the applicant's depositor or creditor status, or from other custodians of the applicant's U.S. real property or liquid assets. In other words, provide as much verification of the individual's assets and liabilities as possible for the underwriter's evaluation.

Inspections and Medical Requirements

Insurers may require an examination by a U.S. trained doctor at the American embassy in the absence of an established relationship with a local paramedical or other examining facility (or they may insist the client be examined during a visit to the U.S.). The insurers may require that blood and urine specimens be express shipped to a U.S.-based insurance laboratory or use an inspection company qualified to perform investigations outside U.S. borders. If the foreign national client cannot be examined in the U.S., but the application was taken while he was on U.S. soil, the underwriter may be suspicious. After all, you really should have anticipated that an exam would be needed and arranged both the exam and inspection (depending upon the company's practices) before the client left the country.

For those insurers established in international markets, such concerns may not be important. Yet for those insurers who are relatively recent entrants into the new world of global insurance opportunities, it is up to you to help facilitate the successful underwriting of your international clients.

Geriatric Medical Underwriting

Persons over age 65 represent the fastest growing segment in the North American population. They also represent a substantial life insurance market. Twenty years ago, life underwriters seldom saw applicants over age 65. Today, it is not unheard of to be asked to assess the insurability of the parent of a 65 year-old!

Most major diseases become more prevalent with increasing age. The average geriatric applicant has 3.5 chronic diseases! Some, such as osteoarthritis, will have little or no impact on insurability for life insurance. Others can make insurance unobtainable.

Historically, life underwriters tended to be conservative when underwriting older age applicants. However, life expectancy gains have been so dramatic that many specialists in the geriatric market are becoming more aggressive. If you are underwriting a 35 year-old and make a mistake, the odds favor you. Most uninsurable 35 year-olds will outlive the interval of time when early death claims are forwarded to the underwriter's boss! The same is now applicable to 75 year-olds. Common sense used to dictate that there would be more death claims over a shorter interval on geriatric business. Yet with modern medical technologies and a more health-conscious geriatric public, 75 and 80 year-olds are living longer, fuller and more active lives.

Geriatric underwriting was also traditionally conservative because of the potential for antiselection. People who know they are ill are amenable to buying insurance. Producers know this—so do underwriters. The amount of insurance applied for, the avowed purpose of the coverage and the applicant's medical history, must still be scrutinized carefully for the stigma of antiselection.

Most importantly, geriatric underwriting is conservative (or appears that way from your perspective) because illnesses are prevalent. Moreover, these illnesses are often "atypical," with different signs and symptoms than those seen in younger persons. What is underwritten liberally at age 35 must be handled more cautiously over age 65. Hematuria (red blood cells in the urine) is a good example. In young people, the cause of blood in the urine is almost always benign. Not so over age 60, where painless and invisible (microscopic) hematuria, detected on an insurance urinalysis, can be the first sign of kidney or bladder cancer.

It is the rule rather than the exception that older age applicants will be taking both prescription and over-the-counter medications (a situation called "polypharmacy" when the number of medications is excessive). As detailed in Chapter 5, therapeutic drugs might have significant effects on routine screening tests. One of the most common errors made by producers in the geriatric market is that they fail to emphasize to older clients the importance of telling the insurance examiner *the precise names of all medications they are taking*.

Here are constructive steps to avoid problems and complications during medical underwriting of geriatric clients.

- **The medical history is apt to be long and complicated. Take a preliminary history during the fact finding interview. Discuss unusual impairments with an underwriter *before preceding*.**

Make sure the examiner records the history accurately. Use cover letters and statements over your client's signature to amplify wherever necessary.

- The APS report is a key (many would say *the* key) requirement. Make sure records from specialists are sought out where necessary to augment the main report from the usual attending physician. Encourage more (not less) detail in the text of the report. Copies of test reports, biopsy pathology reports, etc., are essential. Failure to include them usually means a delay while they are sought with the second inquiry to the physician.

- Discuss the matter of medications with your client during the fact finding interview. Explain the importance of dutifully disclosing all medications, whether prescribed or purchased without a prescription (over-the-counter). Also, ask about other remedies. Some alternative medical practices, such as the use of herbs, might have important implications in the underwriting process.

- Electrocardiograms (ECGs) are commonly required on older applicants. Many times, the significance of an ECG abnormality may be linked directly to how long it has been present. That means the underwriter might be able to be more liberal if historic ECG tracings can be obtained for home office review. If there is an ECG-related problem, raising the question of historic ECGs and their accessibility may be a key to a favorable outcome. Ask your underwriter.

Nonmedical Issues

Market conduct issues should be at the top of your list of concerns when selling to senior citizens. Are the people in this market more vulnerable than other age groups? On one hand, especially in upscale markets, many seniors have financial experience and savvy if they have been successful business people during their working years. On the other hand, the emotional toll of the aging process can leave many seniors susceptible to financial scams involving telephone and door to door solicitors. It is critical that any transaction involving the elderly be fully documented by you and that you be as certain as possible that the client fully understands everything about the product during the sales interview.

Among the areas given extra attention by underwriters in the gray market are "activities of daily living" (ADL). Simply put, how many of the basic tasks you personally take for granted, such as cleaning your yard and home, shopping for groceries or balancing your checkbook, are being done by the elderly applicant without assistance? Mature age interviews done by specially trained paramedics and PHI/inspection interviewers will develop details of ADLs for the underwriter. Geriatric exam protocols now check specifically for gait assessment, cognitive vitality and exercise capacity, among other things. Motor vehicle reports showing recent accidents can be an indicator of slowed mental and physical capacities.

Positive factors in geriatric underwriting can be:

- **Physical activities such as regular exercise and participation in avocations.**

- **Social activities that reflect involvement in the community and with family and friends.**

- **Ownership of a pet(s) which strengthens the feeling that one is needed.**

- **Active use of a computer and the Internet which reflects an interest in learning.**

- **Business activities by seniors who have either started a business or remained active in one.**

- **Family history of maternal and paternal longevity, including grandparents and siblings.**

When adult children of elderly applicants initiate the application for life insurance on their parents, underwriters must be concerned with potential adverse selection. If the adult child wants to be the owner of the policy also, many insurers will decline to participate unless there are clear and unmistakable estate tax reasons for such an arrangement. It may seem unthinkable that an adult child would not act in his elderly parents' best interests, but the realities of human nature demonstrate otherwise.

Many adult children of older age applicants find themselves sandwiched between teenagers entering college and elderly parents needing care and attention. These adults might be working long hours under great strain or they might be in financial distress because of the loss of a job and a reduction in income. When people are desperate, they sometimes do desperate things. Even if physical abuse of an elderly parent is not a risk, verbal and psychological abuse most certainly are. The elderly are already vulnerable because of their aging bodies and often diminished mental agility. They might be emotionally incapable of dealing with strained relationships with their own adult children.

If the elderly applicant has accumulated wealth, and estate taxes would significantly erode those assets, the adult child might be motivated out of self-interest to obtain life insurance on his parent. If the elderly applicant has become a physical, psychological or financial dependent of the adult child, life insurance can be seen as a reimbursement for the monetary and emotional expense visited upon the adult child.

Ideally, the elderly applicant will have made the purchase decision by himself and be the owner of the policy, or have set up a trust that will own the policy. Any circumstance where the elderly applicant is not the decisionmaker must be convincingly explained to the underwriter with adequate supporting documentation.

Survivorship products (joint and second to die) have become recognized as having more exposure to "contagion" risk than previously thought. That is, elderly couples who need such products to protect their substantial assets from tax burdens typically lead an active retired lifestyle involving frequent travel together. Accidental death to one almost inevitably means simultaneous death or serious injury to the other.

In addition, when an elderly wife predeceases her husband, the husband's life expectancy drops. On the other hand, when a husband predeceases a wife, there is little or no adverse impact on the wife's life expectancy unless she was an active caregiver fighting her own illnesses. Elderly females seem to be more emotionally and physically resilient than males.

When submitting a survivorship product application on a couple where the wife is an impaired risk, you should be prepared for the underwriters to be more cautious than usual. If both applicants are impaired risks, or one is uninsurable, the product pricing may limit the underwriter's options for issue. Know the insurer's practices ahead of time and have alternative options of your own to recommend to your clients.

Long-Term Care

This is a health insurance product, whether issued as a stand-alone policy or as a benefit rider on a life or disability policy. However, there is less likelihood of multiple claims than under other casualty products. That is, once benefits begin under a long-term care (LTC) product, they are likely to continue until the death of the insured. Unfortunately, most sales continue to be in the near or already retired markets. As a result, those clients tend to have more complicated medical histories to evaluate.

The policy provisions of LTC policies have continued to evolve as the 21st century begins. This is an immature marketplace that is being monitored closely by regulators and legislators. Some insurers still only pay benefits if the insured is institutionalized, but more are beginning to pay a benefit for home health care. These differences will affect the way underwriters evaluate the risk.

For example, if the activities of daily living would seem to be minimally affected by a purely physical disability risk (i.e., arthritis), there might be a greater likelihood of home health care payments than institutional confinement. On the other hand, if mental acuity (i.e., Alzheimer's) or advanced disability (i.e., severe stroke) are the risks involved, then there is a greater likelihood of institutional confinement. The extent of the performance of activities of daily living (ADL) and instrumental activities of daily living (IADL) will be examined carefully by the long-term care underwriter.

You must understand the provisions of the LTC product you are recommending to your client in order to fully anticipate how the underwriters will evaluate the risks they are being asked to assume.

Critical Illness (Dread Disease) Insurance

In South Africa, Australia, New Zealand, Asia and Europe, these products have been widely and successfully marketed for many years. There is growing list of good reasons to believe that they will become increasingly popular in North America in the years ahead.

- **Longer life expectancies and healthier life-sytyles have decreased interest in *all cause of death* life insurance.**

- **Aging baby boomers are becoming more interested in retirement planning, but retain a logical interest in coverage for those critical illnesses they are most at risk for developing.**

- **The growth of genetic testing in clinical medicine will give more people more knowledge of their personal mortality risks and encourage the purchase of insurance by those who know they are predisposed to a specific critical illness.**

These products work somewhat like the accelerated death benefit riders that became popular on life policies in the U.S. in the wake of AIDS. They pay a benefit if the insured is diagnosed with certain serious, potentially life-threatening illness (cancer, coronary artery disease, etc.). A list of specific covered illnesses is set forth in the policy.

Obviously, critical illness underwriters focus their evaluations on those medical histories that present specific risk under the terms of the policy. When they do encounter factors directly or indirectly bearing on such risks, they have much less leeway for liberalities as compared to life underwriters. Moderate overweight or borderline hypertension, which may be underwritten liberally for life insurance, might compel an extra premium charge for critical illness coverage.

Family history takes on a much larger aspect. Not only will the underwriter be very meticulous about the cause *of* death and the age *at* death of parents and siblings, but he will also pay close attention to the age of onset of covered diseases which have befallen first degree relatives of the proposed insured. Indeed, some adverse family histories will rule out insurability for this unique product.

Individuals previously diagnosed with one of the covered conditions will seldom be insurable unless they are amenable to accepting a contract which excludes that condition. That is not possible in many cases (heart attack, cancer) because the resultant contract would lack much in the way of practical value for the client.

As is the case with traditional life underwriting, the producer aids his own cause on critical illness applications when he works with the client to make sure that as much information as possible, in as much detail as possible, is provided for the underwriter on the application. It is realistic to expect that the vast majority of critical illness applications can be approved as applied for. This is most likely to be accomplished when the underwriter and the producer are on the same wavelength.

APPENDIX

Editor's Note: As recently as January 2000, co-author John Krinik was still receiving positive feedback about the seven year-old checklist found on the following pages. Despite all the literature written about, and the efforts to deal with, market conduct and compliance, this is perhaps the most important question that each agent must ask himself: "Has everything I've done with this client been in the client's best interest?"

"The Ethical Checklist for Agents and the Application Process"

(This article was originally published as "In the Customer's Best Interest— Part 2.")

by
John J. Krinik

In response to the essay "In the Customer's Best Interest," published in the June 14, 1993 issue of *PROBE*, reader John Marshall Lee, CLU, RHU, People Insurance, Fairfield, Ct., called me to determine if I had, or knew of, a checklist of ethical principles that applied to agents and the application process. I didn't. But it's about time there was one.

	YES	NO	DON'T KNOW
Have I made recommendations that were truly in the customer's best interest?	❏	❏	❏
Have I treated the customer as I would want to be treated if our roles were reversed?	❏	❏	❏
Have I acted ethically with regard to the application and underwriting process?	❏	❏	❏
Have I explained the hazards of replacement, if applicable, and complied with all appropriate regulations?	❏	❏	❏
Have I offered a Conditional or Temporary Receipt and fully explained its terms?	❏	❏	❏
Have I insisted that neither the customer nor myself edit any information from the answers to application and exam questions?	❏	❏	❏
Have I explained the contestability clauses to the customer, especially for material misrepresentation?	❏	❏	❏
Have I encouraged the customer to read the pre-notice, authorization, and informed consent forms?	❏	❏	❏
Have I explained to the customer the safeguards insurers use to protect privacy and confidentiality?	❏	❏	❏
Have I explained to the customer about the inspection, examination, laboratory, and other special test requirements and why insurers need them?	❏	❏	❏
Have I performed a needs analysis based on real economic loss with adequate and convincing documentation of that need for both the customer and the underwriting department?	❏	❏	❏

	YES	NO	DON'T KNOW
Have I explained insurable interest and appropriate insurable human life value when the arrangements requested are unusual?	❏	❏	❏
Have I explained to the customer why and how insurers use risk factors, mortality, and morbidity to determine the premium and insurability?	❏	❏	❏
Have I qualified the premium quoted to the customer as being subject to risk evaluation by the underwriting department?	❏	❏	❏
Have I received an unexpected rate or modification from underwriting and explained to the customer truthfully and to the best of my knowledge how the decision was arrived at?	❏	❏	❏
Have I explained to the customer the post-notification forms, if any, or the applicant's option of discussing medical information with his doctor?	❏	❏	❏
Have I explained to the customer what is necessary for future rate reduction when that option exists?	❏	❏	❏
Have I refrained from subtle or overt criticism of the underwriting process in front of the customer and pursued alternative solutions with the insurer instead?	❏	❏	❏
Have I made every effort to demonstrate how the insurance system is flexible and responsive when availability or affordability for the customer with the original insurer have become a problem?	❏	❏	❏

	YES	NO	DON'T KNOW
Have I chosen to represent insurance companies that assist me and the customer in understanding:			
• the principles of risk classification?	❑	❑	❑
• the contractual importance of application completion?	❑	❑	❑
• the role of informed consent and full disclosure relative to underwriting, and the insurers' respect for the privacy and confidentiality of personal information?	❑	❑	❑

John Lee told me this checklist would serve as a useful tool after an agent was back in the office from a client consultation. There are additional items John would add regarding illustrations. I believe any such checklist primarily helps develop the proper attitude. I'd worry most about answers marked "Don't Know."

In the past, free market philosophy said, "Let the buyer beware." Today, citizens, regulators, and legislators will not tolerate businesses that promise what they can't or won't deliver. Agents must anticipate underwriting at the point-of-sale. At the point-of-delivery, agent, company, and industry credibility will be enhanced.

It's all about trust.

Index